Life in
Renaissance
France

Life in Renaissance France

Lucien Febvre

edited and translated by Marian Rothstein

Harvard University Press
Cambridge, Massachusetts
and London, England

Library of Congress Cataloging in Publication Data

Febvre, Lucien Paul Victor, 1878-1956.
  Life in Renaissance France

  Translation of 5 essays first published in Revue des
cours et conférences and later reprinted in the author's
Pour une histoire à part entière.
  Includes bibliographical references and index.
  CONTENTS: Introduction. — The silhouette. — The quest
for knowledge. — The quest for beauty. [etc.]
  1. France — Civilization — 1328-1600. I. Rothstein,
Marian, 1944-   II. Title.
DC33.3F4 1977   944'.02   77-7454
ISBN 0-674-53175-2 (cloth)
ISBN 0-674-53180-9 (paper)

Contents

v

Foreword
Franklin L. Ford

For several reasons, this book deserves our welcome.
One is that Lucien Febvre has long been relegated to
the group of European scholars honored, but not really
well known, by the English-reading world. As Marian
Rothstein's introduction points out, Febvre's study of
Luther—not the magisterial treatment of Rabelais and
the problem of skepticism in the France of the
1500s—is the only work of his available in English. The book on Luther appeared fifty-five years ago,
but the problem in this case is not a matter of age; it is,
or has been, simply one of paucity.

The second reason for being glad that these essays
are appearing in English is related, albeit inversely, to
widespread interest in the writing Febvre did during
the last quarter-century of his life. Too many people
who do know his scholarship think primarily of those
later years when he and Marc Bloch, and the others
they brought into the camp of the *Annales*, seemed
always to be telling, not showing, us how history ought
to be written. Ironically, it was Bloch's death at the
hands of the Nazis during the Second World War that
may have saved his memory from those programmatic
overtures, focusing attention instead on his brilliant
treatments of feudal society, French rural history, and

the magic of kingship. Now it is Febvre's turn to be read just as a historian. In the chapters to follow, you will see how well he could treat substance, not just discuss its treatment.

Still another cause for gratitude to Ms. Rothstein is that she has given us something all too rare, a significant piece of translation executed by someone with the ability to supply critical editing as well. Recent examples of this art, just in the field of early modern European history, include the translation by R. R. Palmer of Georges Lefebvre's *The Coming of the French Revolution* and Nancy Roelker's edition of the journal of Pierre de l'Estoile. There are other instances, of course, but never enough of them.

Perhaps the most important reason for wanting this book, however, is that it makes an important contribution to our knowledge of the French sixteenth century. Despite the existence of useful monographs published in France and a few more general surveys, such as Boulenger's, there is still cause for perplexity about the relative thinness of the work of French scholars in that field, as contrasted with, to cite obvious instances, the middle ages or the seventeenth century. In this country, Russell Major's studies of the estates general and Walter Kaiser's *Praisers of Folly* are among several works that give America some claim to distinction in the field of French Renaissance history. Still speaking only in relative terms, however, one cannot fail to be struck by the curious gap left us by otherwise highly productive generations of historians.

Edmond Esmonin, the distinguished chronicler of Dauphiné and assistant of Ernest Lavisse in the early 1900s, once said to me that his master, in overseeing what stands as the greatest collaborative national history ever put together, almost despaired of having the

sixteenth century treated at what he considered the
requisite level of distinction. It is no disparagement of
either Henry Lemonnier or Jean H. Mariéjol, who
finally produced the volumes in question, to observe
that their editor-in-chief's misgivings were well
founded. Scholars working on the period simply did
not have the footings, in documentary editions and
secondary treatments, to match those on which Lu-
chaire and Langlois could build for medieval segments
of that series, or the bases on which Lavisse himself relied in his own volumes on the age of Louis XIV. That
being so, the ensuing essays by Febvre, written when
he was in his forties, at the peak of his powers, offer
invaluable insight into what has remained, stubbornly,
the least understood part of France's history over the
past eight hundred years.

Ms. Rothstein, in her introduction, covers the principal features of the author's career. Little more need
be said concerning his contributions to the religious
history of the Reformation, his feeling for the provinces (beginning, in his case, with Spanish rule in the
Franche-Comté), or his fruitful meeting with Marc
Bloch at the University of Strasbourg. It might be
pointed out that there must have been some connec-
tion between the lively concern this Frenchman
brought to the presence of Spain in the eastern march
of Burgundy, on the one hand, and, on the other, his
later discovery with Bloch that another hybrid province of France—Alsace—inspired original ways of
considering history. Where better could a student of
the Reformation in both Germany and France flex his
dimensions?

Let me close with just two suggestions. One is that
whoever loves history for its own sake is bound to find
in this book some striking examples of concreteness, of

sensual detail—literally using all five senses—and of
the feeling of recaptured life that comes only with a
skillful call upon that quality. This may be especially
worth saying here, because, as noted above, Febvre is
all too often seen as the theorizer and generalizer, the
cofounder of the *Annales,* methodological preacher
of a history seemingly grown unsure of itself in its
deference to the newer social sciences. Any such char-
acterization is, in my opinion, at best a caricature. The
distortion it contains is revealed in these essays by our
author's love of the specific, the tangible, and not least,
the changing in documented human experience—all
of them familiar features of the historian's landscape.
At times, as even his admiring translator will point
out, he may have ridden certain general themes too
hard. The fifth of the essays presented here, the one
concerning Renaissance merchants, is in my view the
least sensitive, in its hammering at one of Febvre's
favorite points, the "rise of the middle class." Still,
even that chapter offers much that is vivid and suggestive. Taken together, the five pieces constitute a
remarkable achievement in their vicarious recovery of
the past.

What Febvre appears to have grappled with, much
of the time, was the question of continuity and change.
Did he or did he not want to accept a portrayal of
human nature as essentially constant across the centuries, perhaps modified in some respects by the tribal
evolution of Western European man, but never basically altered? Another way to pose the issue would be
to recall the late Carl Becker's frequent reminder to
his seminar at Cornell University, namely, that we all
must decide which of two propositions, both undeni-
ably true, is the more important for the historian. One
is that things change, but change slowly; the other,

that things may change slowly, but do change. Up to a point, I conclude, Lucien Febvre endorsed the former of the two, partly as a warning to "social engineers" that the human race is unlikely to be transformed, at a stroke, beyond all future recognition of its most intractable, if not always its most congenial, characteristics. In these essays, however, he keeps pointing out that people really *do* change in the course of time. He insists that we can recognize sixteenth-century ideals of beauty and knowledge, faith and security, but that the student of history must make an informed and empathetic effort in order to think his way back into the actual meaning of those ideals for the French Renaissance, which is to say back into a reality long since departed.

Both to readers who would like to come closer to the elusive world of France almost five hundred years ago and to those who on balance prefer to emphasize wide-ranging issues posed by history as a discipline, I commend the volume in hand.

Introduction

Lucien Febvre (1878–1956) is probably the most influential French historian of the twentieth century. Most of his books are about the sixteenth century: *Philippe II et la Franche-Comté* (1912); *Un Destin: Martin Luther* (1922); *Le Problème de l'incroyance au seizième siècle: la religion de Rabelais* (1942); *Origène et Des Periers ou l'énigme du "Cymbalum Mundi"* (1942); *Autour de "l'Heptaméron," amour sacré, amour profane* (1944). Of these, only *Martin Luther* has been translated into English, by Roberts Tapley (New York, 1929).

The practice of history represents only one side of Febvre, however, for he was equally a working historian and a crusader, preaching the kind of history he practiced. He believed that the questions which ought properly to concern a historian include all problems suggested by human existence. In 1929, shortly after the essays in this volume were composed, Febvre and Marc Bloch, then both professors of history at the University of Strasbourg, founded a journal, the *Annales d'histoire économique et sociale* (since 1946 the *Annales: Economies, Sociétés, Civilisations*). The journal was to have a major impact in encouraging historical inquiry that cut across the boundaries of history narrowly conceived into social science, psychology, ethnology, not

xiii

to mention more traditional extensions into philosophy, law, literature, and the arts. Febvre worked unceasingly to spread the idea of this kind of history, not only in his own books, but also in lectures and in the articles and reviews he wrote for both the *Annales* and other journals, pieces that generally became platforms, in fact sometimes soapboxes, for his views. In 1953, near the end of his life, he collected a number of these articles, reviews, and lectures to be published as *Combats pour l'histoire,* a title he felt expressed his sense of being engaged in a struggle, a fight for history as he believed it should be. Febvre's importance, for his contemporaries and for the future, lies in his work as a theoretician of history as much as in his efforts as a historian.

History as taught at the end of the nineteenth century, during his school years, seemed to Febvre to be largely a collection of petty details, of diplomatic and political events, one following the other in neat sequence, each effect tidily connected to its cause. Febvre's history is rarely if ever neat, for it starts with a question, and in working toward the answer, often ends with a new question. It is not neat because Febvre recognizes the presence of the individual and the specific, always present and waiting to challenge or undermine the neat generalization repeated for generations and accepted as dogma. It is not neat because he often leaves the process of historical investigation visible in his text, in the belief that making the rough places smooth might also make them less faithful to the truth. Anachronism is the greatest enemy of the historian, who must always fight against the tendency to assume that things then were as things are now: "Be it a matter of prices, horses, feelings, or ideas, no! at four hundred years' distance in societies such as ours, things which continue to be designated by the same word are never the same. To be able, to dare, to compare them one must first know them and evaluate them by themselves—if one can" (*Pour une histoire à part entière*). This attitude demands the use of the techniques of many disciplines, which the historian will use to try to answer the questions posed by the past. Literature and cultural manifestations, unwritten as well as written sources, are as much the province of the historian as are archives or memoirs. New questions are suggested by this approach to history; the need arises for a history of feelings, of how people at a given time think, how their minds work. Febvre was among the first to raise and deal with such questions, questions which remain one of the major concerns of modern historiography.

The essays which follow demonstrate all the major tendencies of Febvre's work. Faced with traditional categories, he refuses to make traditional assumptions. The court of France is not merely a glittering, glamorous place but, upon examination, a constantly traveling group following the king all around the kingdom. History embraces all of life, and so we are reminded to consider the simplest, most down-to-earth aspects of life: people were cold in winter, even indoors. He asks questions about people's feelings, questions which might seem too obvious, too eternal, too incapable of being changed by time to be worth asking—for example, how people felt about their families. The answers are to be found in journals and memoirs. In an age when half of all children died before the age of puberty, when many women died in childbirth and many men died in wars or more local squabbles, people might well regard the members of their families as transitory. Finally, history for Febvre proceeds by anecdote because the anecdote preserves the relationships, the structure, of the time and place under study. The task of the historian is to choose the anecdote, highlight the telling detail, ask the right questions.

Febvre believed that the historian must always approach his evidence with a hypothesis firmly in mind. His success with this technique, his skill in drawing maximum impact from an anecdote, can be illustrated by a few examples. In the first essay below Febvre quotes a letter from the Venetian ambassador to France: "My tenure as ambassador lasted forty-five months . . . I traveled constantly . . . Never during that time did the court remain in the same place for as long as two weeks." However, the full text of the ambassador's letter read as follows:

> My tenure as ambassador lasted forty-five months, during which I traveled constantly. Shortly after my arrival in Paris the king left for Marseille. During a heat wave we crossed the Bourbonnais, the Lyonnais, Auvergne, and Languedoc before coming to Provence. The meeting with the Pope was put off so long that, although everyone expected it to take place in the summer, they finally met in November. Ambassadors who had brought only summer clothing were forced to buy something suitable for winter. The price of furs rose by 50 percent. During the trip I lost a horse and a mule. From Marseille we went through Provence and Dauphiné, the Lyonnais, Burgundy, and Champagne, to Lorraine where the king met the Landgrave of Hesse. Then we returned to Paris . . . When I found myself once again in the Venetian embassy, the stable burned and we lost eleven horses and their harnesses. Only my mule was saved . . . That same

year, as the king wanted to leave, I was forced to buy ten more horses just at the moment when the king called his men to arms and reviewed them on horseback, which raised the price of horses enormously. As I received no subsidy from your Serenity, I was forced to sell some of my silver. Never during the time I was ambassador did the court remain in the same place for as long as two weeks.

Febvre was not distracted by the point of the Venetian's letter, the ambassador's elaborate plea for money. He focused only on the essential, the evidence of the endless travels of the court, which responded to his hypothesis, his question of the moment.

In the same way Febvre read the story of an illegitimate son (conceived while his mother's husband, a merchant, was away on a ten-year business trip), who was taken along as an adolescent on the merchant's next trip and sold into slavery by the merchant (his adoptive father). The storyteller's outline of the merchant's absences become evidence for Febvre of the sixteenth-century merchant's taste for travel (essay 5); the rest of the story is completely discarded. A final example can be mentioned briefly since the source text is readily available in English: to compare Erasmus' version of the story of the four pilgrims with the story as Febvre tells it (at the end of essay 1) is highly instructive of Febvre's unfailing sense of purpose.

Throughout his life, and of course in these essays as well, Febvre was a salesman for his kind of history. His solid grounding in the thought and reality of the sixteenth century is unquestionable. Sometimes, however, the instincts of the salesman, the propagandist, take precedence over the instincts of the scholar. In the interest of driving home a point, the point may be overstated. Sometimes too he sins in the direction of dogma, of hypothesis, for another of his beliefs was that one cannot simply look at the facts; they will speak to the historian only when he comes to them—documents, works of art, works of literature—with specific questions designed to test a hypothesis. In this way, for example, although his observations about the art of the period covered by these essays are accurate, the degree to which they are made subservient to a hypothesis concerning the rise of the middle class may be excessive.

Such minor faults are hugely overshadowed by Febvre's great virtues, his erudition, his ability to question traditional assumptions, and most of all perhaps, his rare talent for finding the telling detail, for composing the scene which will enable the modern reader to leave his own world for the moment and come to understand the world of the past truly on its own terms. The reader who has been exposed to such an experience can then go on to approach other artifacts of the sixteenth century better equipped to see them, not only with his own eyes but also with the eyes of their makers and of those for whom they were made. This is the gift of discovery which Febvre offers in these essays.

A Note on the Translation

The translation is of the complete French text, published first in the *Revue des cours et conférences,* nos. 11 (15 May 1925), pp. 193–210; 12 (1 June 1925), pp. 326–340; 13 (15 June 1925), pp. 398–417; 15 (15 July 1925), pp. 578–593; 23 (15 December 1921), pp. 57–65; 24 (30 December 1921), pp. 143–157; and reprinted in *Pour une histoire à part entière* (Paris, 1962), pp. 528–603 and 428–453. The essays are translated and printed here with the permission of the Service des Publications of the Ecole Pratique des Hautes Etudes, VIe Section. The first four essays were written as a series, while essay 5 examines a closely related topic.

As a translator my aim has been to produce something as close as possible to what Febvre might have written at the moment these essays were composed had he happened to be an English speaker. For this reason the English text is slightly less rhetorical than the French, since the general style and tone of ordinary written English tends to be less rhetorical than a corresponding passage in French. The French conception of the sentence also differs from the English. Compare the five sentences I have used (p. 97) to render Febvre's one: "Un type moral et intellectuel du marchand s'esquisse de bonne heure, avec netteté et précision dans la littérature du temps: celui que nous présente déjà, au début de la dix-neuvième nouvelle, l'auteur des *Cent Nouvelles Nouvelles,* lorsqu'il met en scène ce bon et riche marchand de Londres, d'un coeur si 'atrempé' et d'un courage si vertueux que, mû par 'ardent désir de voir pays, savoir et cognoistre plusieurs expériences qui par le monde universel journellement adviennent,' il s'en va d'abord, bien fourni d'argent comptant et 'de très grande abondance de marchandises,' demeure cinq ans en courses, revient auprès de sa femme, mais, bientôt, repris par la nostalgie de sa vie errante, s'en reva à l'aventure en estrange terre, tant de Chrestiens que de Sarrasins, et ne demoure pas si peu que les dix ans ne furent passez ains que sa femme le revist. . . .'" The ellipses found in the text are Febvre's stylistic device, most often as an appeal to the reader to consider the ramifications of the matter at hand.

The notes which are Febvre's are marked [LF]. I have verified nearly all of these, and provided fuller bibliographical references in some cases and page numbers in many. All other notes are mine; they are designed for several purposes. For instance, Febvre assumes his audience has passed through the French school system (which, it should be remembered, is nationally uniform). English speakers may well be unfamiliar with battles or noblemen Febvre refers to in passing, often apparently meant to evoke recollections of long-past schoolroom lessons. I have tried to smooth over this difference in backgrounds with notes. Whenever possible, references are given to English translations or to alternate books available in English. References to classics, for example, Rabelais or Michelet, are given by title and chapter so that any edition, and in the case of Rabelais, any translation, may serve. In fields in which considerable work has been done since Febvre wrote these essays, I have attempted to expand the notes with references to specific works and pertinent information drawn from them. Occasionally, led on by Febvre's own tendency for such things, a note offers some supplementary piece of concrete contemporary evidence.

M.R.
Madison, Wisconsin

I

The Silhouette of a Civilization

Littré, in his *Dictionary* of 1873, calls civilization "the condition of that which is civilized; it is the body of opinions and customs formed by the interaction of technology, religion, arts and sciences." Civilization is a product: the product of moral, material, intellectual, and religious forces acting on the human consciousness in a given place and at a given time.[1] Littré, in spite of the inelegance of his own definition, would certainly agree. Holding firmly to this idea, we shall in the pages to come by no means attempt to examine or reconstruct "the body of opinions and customs" on which a society as varied and alive as that of early Renaissance France was based. Nor shall we imitate the bustling host who does not let his Sunday visitors leave before he has shown them every rabbit in the hutch and each and every cabbage in the patch. We shall limit ourselves to essentials, to what was truly characteristic of the highest and most original parts of that civilization which we still admire today. We shall seek out all that which best defines the highest aspirations and commitments of the people of that time, the people who lived through and made the Renaissance, Humanism, and the Reformation, their strivings after Knowledge, Beauty, and God. That will be the subject of this study.

All those admirable efforts share a common ground: man's image of himself. History is the study of man. In his glorious *Introduction*,[2] Michelet congratulates himself for having given history so fine and firm a basis: the earth. He was quite right. But on that foundation, as stable as it is varied, we must set men. Renaissance, Humanism, Reformation are not mere abstractions, personifications wandering over the heavens where the Chimera chases Transcendent Ideals. To understand these great changes we must recreate for ourselves the habits of mind of the people who brought them about.

Were those minds like our minds? I know that man's essential nature is unchanging through time and space. I know that old tune. But that is an assumption, and I might add, a worthless assumption for a historian. For him, as for the geographer, as we have had occasion to remark earlier, man does not exist, only men.[3] His efforts are directed toward discerning the particular originality, the distinguishing marks, all that in which and by which those men differed from us, men who did not live or feel or behave as we do.

The men of the early sixteenth century must be the object of our attention if we wish to try to understand what the Renaissance was, what the Reformation was. It would be an impossible task to try to "recreate" them, to build them up into their real unity, an impossible task and an unnecessary one. Let us be less ambitious. By way of introduction it should be enough to evoke them, projecting onto the screen of our imaginations some typical silhouettes. Looking at these images now will prove helpful later when, having seen, we try to understand.

Twentieth-century man, the Frenchman of the twentieth century, can be defined in many ways, but essentially, taken in terms of his physical existence, his material life, three points stand out: he is urban, sedentary, and refined. We are urban, living an urban life in the city, the modern big city which is not merely a place where there is a greater agglomeration of people more densely packed than elsewhere, but a place where man is not the same as elsewhere. Age distribution, for example, is not the same in the city as in the country. Proportionally there are fewer children and fewer old people than adults, who, having spent their childhood elsewhere, often leave the city in retirement, adults who come to the city to spend the strength of their youth and their maturity. All ties between us and the land have been broken, except perhaps for a short time during vacations. The land seen through urban eyes is a place of rest and relaxation and beauty rather than hard physical labor.

We are sedentary. We may talk much about travel and go rushing about by car or by plane; that is only further proof of our need to be sedentary. The ever-increasing speed of such machines, their flexibility, their ease of access, in fact, the comfort they provide, make it possible for us to take long trips without ever really leaving home. How rare it is nowadays to find the ordinary man more than two or three days' journey from his home.

Man has become urban, sedentary, and refined as well. What a large place the word "comfort" has come to occupy in our language, modern comfort in which we take such pride. What implications the word has, of convenience and material ease: a light turned on or off at the flick of a finger, an indoor temperature independent of the seasons, water ready to flow hot or cold, as we wish, anytime, anywhere. All these, and a thousand other marvels as well, fail to astonish us. Yet they affect the physical temper of our bodies, help us to avoid certain diseases and make us prey to others. They influence our work habits, our leisure time, our customs and conventions, and all the ways of thinking and feeling which are the result of these things. Can we really claim then that they are merely exterior, merely accident, not worth noting or discussing? We are tied to all this technology, it has a hold on us, it makes us serve it, odd, rooted spirits as we are. We are slaves three times over to the insatiable hungers we ourselves have created. In that sense, the men of the sixteenth century were free.

I

The people who lived in the sixteenth century, in the France of Charles VIII, of Louis XII, of François I, were not urban; they lived on the land. There were no big cities in the modern sense of the word. It is true that foreigners, and the French themselves, sang the praises of their cities. They spoke of Paris as one of the wonders of the world. Yet what were these cities really like? We see the sixteenth-century city laid out before us in old prints, in cosmographies, in collections of maps: Munster, Belleforest, Antoine du Pinet, Braun and Hogenberg.[4] The city lay surrounded by crenelated walls, flanked by round towers. A sunken road led to the narrow gate protected by a drawbridge guarded night and day by watchful soldiers. To the right, a crude cross. Straight ahead on a hill top, a huge gibbet, pride of the citizens, where the bodies of hanged men were left to mummify. Often over the gate, impaled on a spike, hung a head or an arm or a leg, some hideous slice of human flesh carved by the hangman: justice at work in a thick-skinned society.

The sunken road leading to the gate was muddy.

Past the gate the street widened as it followed a capricious route through the town. A filthy stream ran down its center, fed by rivulets of liquid manure seeping from nearby manure heaps. It was a muddy slough in the rain, a desert of choking dust in the heat of the sun, in which urchins, ducks, chickens, and dogs, even pigs in spite of repeated edicts to control them, all wallowed together.

Entering the city we see that each family has its own house, as in the country. As in the country, each house has a garden behind it, where boxwood borders mark out the vegetable patches. And again as in the country, because city life is the barest modification of country life, each house has an attic with a window for raising and storing hay, straw, grain, and all kinds of winter provisions. Each house has its oven where the mistress and the female servants bake every week. Each house has its press near the cellar, filled every October with the fumes of new wine. Finally, each house has its stable with saddle and draft horses, and its barn with cows and oxen and sheep, led away in the morning when the neighborhood shepherd blows his horn, and brought home again in the evening.

The city was permeated by the country. The country even penetrated into the houses. The city man received his country tenants in his home, peasants who came periodically, bringing their master what his land had produced, laying baskets heavy with their rustic bounty on the polished tiles of the floor. The lawyer received his clients in his study, their arms filled with hares and rabbits, chickens or ducks.[5] The country penetrated city bedrooms in the summertime. when the floor was strewn with flowers or leaves and the unused fireplaces were filled with greenery to keep the rooms cool and sweetsmelling. In the winter the floor tiles were covered with a thick layer of country straw to help keep men and animals warm. The country made its presence felt even in everyday language, which was filled with allusions to the fields. Seasons began with the singing of the cricket, the blooming of the violet, the ripening of the wheat. The city, filled with orchards, gardens, and green trees, was nothing but a slightly more densely populated countryside. Life there was scarcely more rushed or more complex than in the villages. The city had no hold on its inhabitants.

II

The great majority of people did not live in cities. Nor were all those who lived on the land peasants. All the noblemen of France in those days had homes in the country.[6] Some of them lived in chateaux, often admirable buildings. But let us turn away for a moment from the classsical façades, the sculptures, the finely carved marble, and look instead at these fine houses with the eye of a prospective tenant. Each room leads to the next, all huge, all monotonously square: a wall in front, a wall behind, windows in the left wall, windows in the right. To go from one end of the house to the other, one must pass in turn through all the rooms in the series. This was not only the case in France. In his diverting *Memoirs,* Benvenuto Cellini explains the rather colorful origin of the disfavor in which he tells us he was held by the Grand Duchess of Tuscany. When Cosimo dei Medici in his palace in Florence sent for his favorite sculptor, Benvenuto Cellini had to drop whatever he was doing and rush to his master. Quickly, nearly running, he would burst through the door and climb the stairs. On his way to see the Duke he would go from room to room, crossing

each in turn. But these rooms were not all merely cere-
monial chambers; there were also private ones, even
very private ones used by the Grand Duchess herself.
And from time to time it happened that these rooms
were not empty when he passed through them, so that
the artist was forced, in passing, to bow before some
noble and powerful person whose attention at that moment was fully occupied with other things, and to
whom the sudden appearance of the artist in these
most private apartments must have seemed highly dis-
agreeable. But Cellini had no choice; the Grand Duke
was waiting and this was the only possible route.[7]

That took place in Florence, in the Uffizi, in
Florence which by comparison with France at the
same time was a model of delicacy and refinement.
Now consider what the real level of comfort in a
French chateau must have been. For one thing, people
must have lived through the winter shivering, their
teeth chattering. We may admire the huge fireplaces
which sometimes extend over the whole of one wall of
the great square rooms, and we are quite right to do so.
We are in a position to admire them, standing as
tourists in the chateau where central heating has since
been installed. In the sixteenth century they were also
admired, but the people who did so kept their fur-
lined coats and their warm hats on. In vain did an
army of woodcarriers bring in load after load of
branches and logs to be added to fire after fire. All the
brightly burning (or smoking) fireplaces of Chambord
or Blois would not meet the requirements of us modern sybarites. Far from the fire it was freezing; and
when the flames crackled and rose, close to the fire it
was hot enough to fry you. People were cold, always
cold, even inside their homes.[8]

Their homes were simply an extension of the countryside, without the sharp contrast of home's welcoming warmth. Can we really believe that the ideas of such people about home and hearth, about the family, would be the same as those held today by people drunk with warmth, slaves to central heating? Now try for a moment to imagine modern man without any ideas or feelings about his house, his home. What a void this would create! In fact, thinking about what those palaces were really like, one may find oneself, timidly, speaking the words of Brother Lardoon, the monk from Amiens who went to Florence with Epistemon: "These things carved from marble and prophyry are beautiful; I have nothing against them. But the pastries of Amiens, the old roast shops with the mouthwatering odors, and, yes, even the girls there . . . ."[9] Those good everyday, useful, comfortable things have their worth after all, a very considerable one.

III

In any case, the list of such chateaux is short: Blois, Chenonceaux, Azay, Amboise, Oiron, Bonnivet. They are the exception. The ordinary dwelling for the gentleman who was not a prince was a manor house. And in the manor, people spent most of their time in a single room, the kichen.[10] Generally, meals were eaten there. (French houses almost never had a special room for dining until the eighteenth century. Even Louis XIV, on ordinary occasions, ate his meals at a square table placed in front of the window in his bedroom. The noblemen of the sixteenth century, having fewer pretentions, generally ate in the kitchen.) This room is called, in the dialect of some provinces, the "heater." That is the giveaway. It was warm in the kitchen, or at

least, less cold than elsewhere. There was always a
fire. The aromatic steam coming from the stew-pot
made the air a bit heavy perhaps, but warm, and all
told, welcoming. Fresh straw spread on the floor kept
people's feet warm. People gathered in the kitchen
where they lived elbow to elbow, and they relished
this kind of closeness. Like all peasants, they hated to
be alone. The more the merrier. The sixteenth century
did not have our modesty. It knew nothing of our need
to be alone.[11] The beds of the day are evidence of this,
great big things in which several people would sleep at
once without embarrassment or scruples.[12] Individual
bedrooms are a modern idea. "Whatever for?" our
forefathers would have asked. Setting apart a room for
each activity is another modern notion. The kitchen
was the gathering place for everyone, and everything,
or almost everything, was done there.

The lord of the manor and his wife were there in
their high-backed wooden chairs next to the fire.
Their children, both boys and girls, sat on benches.
Their guests were received there, the parish priest,
their tenants, and their servants. Bustling servants
laid or cleared the table under the vigilant eye of their
mistress. Farmers, plowmen, day laborers coming in
from the fields at day's end heavy with fatigue and
with mud, sank into their seats to eat their meager
fare. Adding to the confusion were the animals:
chickens and ducks who made their home beneath the
table, hunting birds perched on the shoulders of the
hunters, dogs crouched at their masters' feet, grooming
themselves as they lay stretched out in the straw or
searching out their fleas under the cover of the women's
skirts or roasting themselves before the fire.

Slowly, methodically, respectfully, people ate the
coarse food put before them. Bread was rarely made

from wheat.[13] Thick floury soup, mush made of millet or groats were served in place of potatoes or pasta.[14] Generally each person at the table was given a large thick slice of somewhat stale dense bread.[15] On this, using three fingers, the diner scooped up whatever he might choose from the central serving dish.[16] Very little red meat was eaten except at weddings and other special occasions. Salt pork appeared from time to time, but there were many meatless days, and fast days, and days of abstinence, and Lent so well, so strictly observed that people often undermined their health.[17] When there was meat it was game or fowl. The sixteenth century did not know the stimulation provoked by red meat, by flesh food accompanied by alcohol and wine; it did not know the illusion of strength and power which modern man obtains from his usual food, nor the instant stimulation of the nervous system which, thanks to coffee, even the most humble know today. The closest equivalent in the sixteenth century was spices, whose use was limited only by their enormous cost. People who used neither alcohol nor tobacco nor coffee nor tea and who only rarely ate red meat got their stimulation from spices, setting themselves aflame with ginger and pepper and nutmeg and carefully concocted mustards.[18]

All told, people spent very little time in the house. They came to eat or to take refuge when life and work in the fields was cut short by a heavy rain, and at night. Night too was different; man had not yet learned to conquer the darkness. The kitchen and bedrooms were lit most usually by the dancing flames in the fireplace. Lamps were, in general, nasty, sooty little things which sputtered or smoked and spread their stench through the room. We can scarcely imagine what one of those big kitchens must have been like after three or four hours of habitation by twenty or so people still in work clothes, not to count the animals who lived there. The room would fill with musty, lingering odors of men and beasts and past meals, the acrid odor of sputtering wicks and the smell of muck-spattered leggings drying in front of the fire. Imagine a boy who wants to settle in his nook to read or to study under such conditions. How can he amidst all this disorder? The kitchen is not for reading except maybe four or five times a year when it is raining hard and no one knows what else to do. As a last resort someone reads aloud a few chapters from an old romance. From time to time, late in the evening when everyone else is in bed, the master brings his account book up-to-date, carefully detailing what was owed him as well as his expenses. Real life for this man and those like him was life out-of-doors, riding over the fields and vineyards, the meadows and woods. They oversaw their land while they hunted or hunted while overseeing their land. Real life was going to a fair or a market, exchanging a few words with the peasants there in a shared language about shared interests which, needless to say, were neither political nor metaphysical. On Sundays and holidays the lord, who considered from a certain point of view was nothing but a kind of superior peasant, started the dance by taking the girls once around the floor, and if need be played at bowls, archery, or wrestling.

IV

But what about the court, you will ask, the brilliant court of François I, if not earlier, that of Charles VIII or Louis XII? Let us have a look at the court. The word itself is impressive, evoking magnificent visions: great gilded rooms glowing with the light of a thousand

11

candles, filled with lords and ladies who themselves live in sumptuous chateaux. It matters little whether we imagine the Louvre, Saint-Germain, Fontaine-bleau, Chambord, or, later, Versailles. Only the outward setting and the fashions change. But the court surely always remains just that, the court, a place of privilege above all, and display, where powerful people, whose every costume costs a fortune, gather to live in ostentatious luxury and comfort in the midst of a continual whirl of banquets, receptions, and other entertainments. Lazy and useless lives no doubt, yet not totally free of all signs of wit, clever remarks, now and then, little verses or biting epigrams.

Very well. But against this image must be set the work of patient scholars who have gathered and classified the letters and documents of the royal chancellery. From these we can reconstruct, day by day, for all the thirty years of the reign of François I, the activities of the sovereign. Suppose we open the collection at random to 1533.[19] The king was just over forty. He was already starting to turn gray; his eyes were becoming heavy; his nose was growing longer. The ladies of Paris and elsewhere had left a heavy mark on the king. And the earlier misfortune of Pavia had broken many an enchantment.[20]

On the first of January, 1533, François I was in Paris, at the Louvre. He had spent all of December there. He was to spend all of January and February there. Three months in the same place! That was most unlike the king's usual habits. He soon reverted to another pattern. In March the king set off. First he made a tour of the Valois and the Soissonais. On the seventh of March he was at La Ferté-Milon; on the ninth at the Abbey of Longpont; on the tenth, at Fère-en-Tarendois; on the fifteenth at Soissons; on the seventeenth at

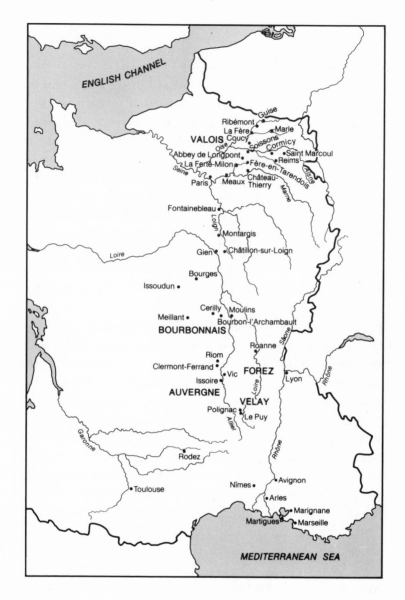

The Travels of the King

The places included in the king's itinerary for 1533 are shown here. The map suggests how much travelers in the sixteenth century relied on rivers, both for transport on their waters and for roads on the flat land along river banks.

Coucy. Then he turned northward. François spent the twentieth at Marle and la Fère; the twenty-first at Ribémont; the twenty-second at Guise; the twenty-fourth at Marle again. Then he turned toward Champagne. On the twenty-eighth he arrived at Saint-Marcoul de Corbeny; the next day he was at Cormicy, and the day following at Reims. That city, in which the kings of France were crowned, did not hold him long. By the third of April he had arrived in Château-Thierry by the way of Fère-en-Tarendois. He stayed there for three days. By the seventh he was at Meaux, but by then it was Holy Week and the king remained at Meaux for the Easter celebrations. It was not until the nineteenth that he came to Fontainebleau to spend a week. On the twenty-sixth he was at Gien, having come by way of Montargis and Châtillon-sur-Loign. Then he set off toward Bourges, arriving on the second of May for three days, after which he set off again toward Moulins where he spent four days after touring the Bourbonnais: Issoudoun, Meillant, Cérilly, Bourbon-l' Archambault. With an intermediate stop at Roanne, the king made his way to Lyon by the twenty-sixth of May. And there he stopped. He spent a month in Lyon, not, of course, without making numerous excursions to other places nearby. At the end of June he left the city, crossed the Forez, and entered Clermont-Ferrand on July tenth. Next he wandered about the Auvergne from Riom to Issoire to Vic. A week later he was in Velay. By the seventeenth he had come as far as Polignac; by the eighteenth he was at le Puy for two days; the twenty-fourth at Rodez; the twenty-fifth on the road to Toulouse, the city where he spent the first week of August. By August ninth he was at Nîmes; on the twenty-ninth he began a twelve-day stay at Avignon; by September fifteenth he was in Arles; the twenty-first at Martigues; the twenty-second at Marignane. On the fourth of October he entered Marseilles. We need follow him no further; it is clear that we shall have had more than enough of these endless lists of dates and places long before François I had his fill of travel. Was this the life of a king or of a knight-errant, wandering always, up hill and down dale? Or a revision of *Don Quixote* by the Flying Dutchman?

The court followed the king. It followed him on the highway, through the woods, along the rivers and across the fields, more like a train of perpetual tourists than a court. Or, more exactly, it was like a troop doing a day's march. The advance party would move out ahead to set up "camp" before the king arrived: the quartermaster, the official charged with finding and allocating housing for everyone; and a whole tribe of cooks, specialists in sauces, roasts, and pastries. Riding old nags usually acquired through the generosity of the king, they hurried through the dawn to that night's stopping place. It might be a simple village house, a gentleman's manor, or the palace of some important nobleman. Or, if need be, from time to time the king would be content to spend the night in the big tent which a sturdy mule bore on its back, following all the peregrinations of the king. The tent might be set up anywhere, in a clearing, in the midst of the fields or meadows, as the whims of the master dictated.[21]

Once the advance party had moved out, the body of the court began to leave also. First the king and his guards, officers, and gentlemen of his household: as he passed through a village the church bells would ring, and the priests would come running to the roadside. The peasants who saw the royal cortege approach from the distance as they worked in the fields would run

toward it. There, in the midst of a splendid group of
mounted men, they saw the king, either on horseback
himself or riding in a litter that lurched with each step
taken by the stout mules drawing it. Behind the king
came the ladies of the court, ladies who did a day's
march alongside the men. Following the example of
the king, they too lived like soldiers on a campaign.
Constant travel may eventually become a way of life
which one comes to enjoy or even to feel a kind of nos-
talgia for; nonetheless it is not an easy life or a restful
one, not suited to frail women of delicate constitution.

The ladies of the court were not frail. Their portraits have been preserved for us thanks to the popularity of pencil drawings in the sixteenth century. Collections of these portraits, especially those of the most
beautiful and powerful figures of the court, drawn
with varying degrees of skill, are to be found in the
most far-flung lands. What disappointments await us
in the pages of such collections. The written words of
contemporaries are filled with a thousand sincere-
sounding compliments. And here are the ladies of un-
paralleled beauty preserved, for example, in the
Montmor collection in the Library at Aix-en-Provence,
once attributed to Madame de Boissy, wife of the head
of the king's household. The portraits have manuscript captions.[22] First we come to Madame de Chateaubriand, mistress of the king, of Bonnivet,[23] and
others too, none of whom was ashamed of the association. She was the devoted sister of Lescun, Lesparre,
and of the ill-starred Lautrec.[24] Looking at the portrait
of so famous a beauty we find a rather fleshy blond
woman with a wide, flat face and rather ordinary
shoulders. The caption leaves us with a shred of hope:
"Formed better by nature than by pencil," it says. We
find Madame de l'Estrange. Her name in the madri-

gals of the day inevitably rhymed with "face d'Ange" (angel face); her face now seems to have been whittled from some cheap, intractable wood. And Diane de Poitiers, who was the delight of the son, Henri II, after having been the joy of the father, François I, surely must have been an extraordinary woman to be able to extend her reign from one sovereign to the next, especially when the two men were so unlike one another. "A beautiful sight, an honest companion," says the caption under her portrait in the Montmor collection. No doubt she was honest, at least in Brantôme's sense.[25] As for her looks, however, we see an astute face with a sharp nose, premature bags under the eyes, and a wide, thin-lipped mouth. This is the evidence not merely of one portrait, but of five of six drawn between 1525 and 1550, so that no effort of the will can make our own esthetic sense coincide with that of our ancestors: for us that face holds neither charm nor distinction nor grace nor beauty.[26]

It is odd that these depictions of great ladies or princesses or court favorites almost never convey a sense of breeding or nobility. Or perhaps what breeding there is seems surprisingly rustic and casual. But in all fairness, how could they have refined their features or simply preserved the freshness of their looks while exposing themselves constantly, on horseback, to the out-of-doors, to the cutting wind, to the driving rain and snow, traveling for weeks and weeks without real rest, without anything more than improvised lodgings? The ladies of the court were a sad sight as they followed the king; the oldest dozing in their litters, the others rocked by the rhythmic step of their mares or packed into wagons without springs so that the wheels transmitted every bump in the road. Relief might come when they all piled into a rented or borrowed

17

barge, to drift between the flat banks of some river or stream.

Twelve thousand horses, three or four thousand men, not counting the women (who were by no means all of the respectable sort): the court was like a little army, privately outfitted, self-sufficient, living an independent existence. It brought its own merchants of all sorts, protected and regulated by the chief provost, granted the sole right to supply the courtiers. There were butchers and poultrymen, fishmongers and greengrocers, fruiterers and bakers; wine merchants prepared to sell both wholesale and retail; purveyors of hay and straw and oats. There was a whole tribe of servants to aid in the hunt: to care for the dogs and falcons; to see to the nets and traps. Another group was needed to see to the feeding of the court: two mares carrying bottles of wine intended for the king's table and that of his chamberlains and the head of his household; cooks and their apprentices who on certain days established by tradition would entertain the king with dances. And there were the couriers and fast riders, hardy horsemen who were always ready to ride at top speed to the nearest coast from the depths of Auvergne or Burgundy, seeking oysters or mussels or fish for the king's table on meatless days.

Ambassadors were brought to despair by the unsettled life of the court. One of them, Mariano Giustiniano, was ambassador in 1535, that is, two years after the period we have just been examining in detail. To the Senate in Venice he wrote the following report: "My tenure as ambassador lasted forty-five months . . . I traveled constantly . . . Never during that time did the court remain in the same place for as long as two weeks."[27] It should be said that of all those who followed the peregrinations of the court, the diplomats suffered the most. The king did his best to avoid contact with these observers, interested by profession in unearthing hidden secrets, and he led them a merry chase in doing so. He was careful never to inform them of the court's itinerary; he would invent a hunt or a sudden excursion as an excuse to flee their company. They, on the other hand, were professionally obliged to be as close as possible to the person of the king.

The nobles were less assiduous. Those who followed the royal party for more than a month or two were rare indeed. Most of those who already belonged to the world of the court came each year to spend a few weeks with the king. They left their land and their homes intending to return, and in fact, they did so as soon as they could. There they recovered and settled once more into a familiar society, while from the north to the south, from the east to the west, from the Ardennes to Provence, from Brittany to Lorraine, the king of France, on horseback, continued his rounds, begun at his coronation and ended by his death.

V

What has been said so far has brought us to no conclusion. No conclusion is wanted, for the aim of these pages has been to present to the reader, by way of introduction, a few images of life in sixteenth-century France, images of the time of Louis XII and François I, striking images. They show us in action, so to speak, people performing timeless acts, going through the eternal circle of all human life. But if I am not entirely mistaken, the reader has also seen, and I suppose felt, as he was reading, that this eternal circle did not follow quite the same course in the sixteenth century as it does today.

Was man in the abstract the same? Possibly. I know nothing about him. He and the historian have little contact, for the historian is concerned with reality rather than abstractions. Concrete man, living man, man in flesh and blood living in the sixteenth century and modern man do not much resemble each other. He was a country man, a nomad, a rustic, and in all these we are far from him. When we see him before us in the strength of his manhood at the age of forty, what dangers has he not surmounted, what challenges has he not overcome? Above all, he survived. He lived through his first sixteen years during which, regularly, at the very least half of all children died.[28] Family account books yield an eloquent record of this grim fact. They are punctuated nearly every three lines by the death of a child, like the tolling of a funeral bell.[29] Later, our sixteenth-century man escaped death by that combination of mortal scourges known in a word as the plague, which killed several thousand people each year, spreading occasionally to epidemic proportions when it would decimate entire populations.

However middle class, however bourgeois, we may assume him to be, however far by profession from arms and the military, he had nonetheless risked his life a hundred times as a soldier. When the enemy was at the gates of his city about to besiege it, he ran to the ramparts with his halberd and his helmet to fight alongside the others. He risked his life equally when he traveled, as all men of the sixteenth century did, whether they were lawyers or merchants or journeymen making their tour of the kingdom, or students heading across the Alps to the schools of Padua or Pavia. They all wrote their wills before leaving home. As he approached the nearby woods, the traveler would observe the dark copse spreading up the hillside, offering a hiding place for the brigand waiting for the opportunity to attack the unaccompanied or unarmed as they passed. In the wretched inn which he reached just as night fell, the exhausted traveler found sinister vagrants and black-handed charcoal burners; men whose motions were brusque and whose faces gave rise to disquieting suspicions came stealthily into the room to drink themselves sodden. The traveler spent the night standing guard in his miserable room, without fire or lamp to give him light, his sword unsheathed and placed across the crude wooden table he had pushed against the door to keep it closed. By dawn he had had enough; he fled without further ado, pleased to find that thieves had not made off with his horse.[30]

Life was a perpetual combat to be waged against man, the seasons, and a hostile and ill-controlled nature. A person who was victor in such a combat, who arrived at maturity without too many accidents or misadventures, had a tough skin, a thick hide, literally as well as figuratively. If a vein of great sensitivity or delicacy lay hidden beneath the surface toughness we have no way of knowing it. History must limit itself to recording appearances. In the sixteenth century, appearances are neither gracious nor soft. One, two, five children in a family died in infancy, carried off by unknown diseases ill-distinguished or ill-diagnosed and generally ill-cared-for. The family record book simply notes the death and the date. Then the writer, father of the child, passes on to more notable events: a hard frost in April killing the autumn's fruit in the bud, an earthquake signaling great catastrophes. His wife might be respected for her virtue and her fecundity, and praised, perhaps, for the skill with which she ran the home. But when she died, leaving her husband too

21

few children, five or six at most, he married again as
soon as he could because it was important to have a
dozen, more if possible. On the other hand, if a peasant
in the country had been left a widow and remarried,
she would not take her children by the first marriage;
they were left to shift for themselves as servants or
beggars by the roadside.[31]

Thomas Platter, in his memoirs, evokes a life enormously far from our own although we are separated
from him by scarcely more than seven or eight normal
lifetimes.[32] Thomas Platter tells us, as though he were
speaking of something entirely ordinary, without
registering the least surprise, that as his father died
when he was still an infant, his mother remarried soon
thereafter. This caused the immediate dispersion of
her children, so that Platter simply did not know how
many brothers and sisters he had. With effort he could
recall the names of two sisters and three brothers and
something of what became of them. About the others
he remembered nothing. He himself was taken in by
an aunt. He never again heard from his mother. This
was, no doubt, the behavior of the people in the wild
Valais. But there is nothing which suggests that the
customs of people elsewhere were any less harsh.

Indeed, the things which are nearest and dearest to
us today—home, hearth, wife, and children—seem to
have been regarded by the man of the sixteenth century as merely transitory goods which he was always
prepared to renounce. On occasion he would renounce
them without any very real or serious reason for doing
so, impelled by an unconscious need to wander, the
sprouting of seeds planted by generations of crusading
and errancy. One of the constant companions of any
historian of the sixteenth century is the *Colloquies* of
Erasmus, a small but rich mirror of the times. In it we

find scenes such as this:[33] Four men are sitting at a table. They are middle-class, peaceful, sedentary, married, well-established men who have come together as old friends to share a glass of wine. Perhaps they have shared a glass too many and the wine has gone to their heads. One of them suddenly bursts out: "Any friend of mine will follow me; I'm going on a pilgrimage to Santiago de Compostella." A drunken impulse. The second man speaks in turn: "As for me, I'm not going to Santiago, I'll go all the way to Rome." The third and fourth friends make peace in the group, suggesting a compromise. First they will go to Santiago and then, from there, to Rome. All four of them will go, and they pass a glass of wine to drink to their pilgrimage. The pact has been sealed, the vows made. There is no going back on it, so they leave. One of the pilgrims dies in Spain; the second in Italy. The third is left dying in Florence by the fourth who returns home alone a year later, worn out, prematurely aged and ruined. The story is not fiction; it depicts the customs of a time which is no longer ours.

These are the things we should try to remember when we wish to understand the "things of the sixteenth century." We must remember that we are all, like it or not, hothouse products; the man of the sixteenth century grew in the open air.

2

The Quest for Knowledge

The words "sixteenth century" immediately call to mind the Renaissance. But what is the Renaissance? What is Humanism? When and where did they begin? What dates shall we set for the Renaissance? Can they be the same for France, Italy, Germany? How did the Renaissance come about, and were there no renaissances before the Renaissance?[1] These are all serious questions worthy of our attention, but a single essay cannot hope to deal with them. So, turning away from theories, questions of principle, and schoolroom controversies, let us look directly to the man of the sixteenth century, homely, lean, nomadic man as he was during the French Renaissance.

What can be seen at first glance on that honest face, hardened by exposure to the four winds, weathered by sun and rain, is above all an enormous stock of good will supported by strong nerves and broad shoulders somewhat stooped by hard work, the peasant's toughness. Imagine now that such a man sets himself to study. What will he become? The answer is obvious: he will be a scholar, that is, such a man will learn all there is to be learned. He will learn with the obstinate fury, the silent determination which the vintner exhibits as he climbs his steeply terraced land for the thousandth time, his basket on his back, beneath the burning sun or the driving rain. He will learn with the determination of the reaper, cutting swath after swath in his field with untiring, rhythmic, timeless motions. A man such as this knows the price of learning: a man of the out-of-doors who inflicts the sedentary labors of study upon himself will treat knowledge with the kind of pious respect which his parents and he himself demonstrated for that holy thing, food, bread, good wheaten bread. As an old man, Viret, who helped to convert the Romanic parts of Switzerland to the cause of the Reformation, recalled that when in his childhood he heard the churchbells ring in Orbe, his native village, he knew very well what message the clappers hammered out against the bells. His mother had revealed their secret to him. The bells of Orbe sang, over and over again, "pain perdu, tu seras battu" [wasted bread, a rap on the head]. Little children walked to school to the interior rhythm of this chant, "pain perdu, tu seras battu, pain perdu, tu seras battu."[2] In the sixteenth century the rustic son of a peasant who had conquered the bread of the spirit by dint of stubborn effort was not the man who would waste so much as a crumb of it. Such a man flung himself into his work holding nothing back. He gave himself to study with such naive faith, such willingness, such absence of ulterior motive as is found in the unsmiling peasant, completely absorbed by his plowing until the task is done.

This outline can be applied to what we all know about the literature and the intellectual life of the sixteenth century. We must be careful not to plunge ahead too quickly, for the real question is what caused such a tough and rustic fellow to study? What motivated him? Above all, the answer is peace.

I

At the end of the fifteenth century and the start of the sixteenth, France enjoyed both prestige and security, things always desired, and relished when found.[3] Victories in Italy at Fornovo, Milan, Novara, Genoa, Agnadello, and Ravenna (with Marignano to come a bit later) brought France a full measure of military glory.[4] From the depths of their tombs the barons of days past, the old crusaders, must have swelled with pride. And they found their like, their equal, in La Tremoille, Gaston de Foix, Trivulzio, and above all, Bayard.[5] These epic heroes were all the more admired for the fact that their exploits took place far from France. Within the changing frontiers gallantly maintained in Italy, French merchants and French peasants worked on.

They had their work cut out for them. English invasions, the depredations of soldiers and highwaymen, and later, the pitiless despotism and the merciless taxation under Louis XI, year after year after year, had crushed a dwindling population. In the France of 1470, and still in 1480, there were ruins everywhere, uncultivated fields, abandoned and burnt villages. Wolves prowled in the brush, and among the decaying houses the empty shell of the church lay like a corpse, its sides caved in, its soul gone from the body.[6] For thirty years, until under Louis XII, everywhere there was peace, riches, abundance. New houses, new churches, new chateaux appeared on the land.[7] Life was happy, life was gay, life was for eating and laughing and dancing. Peace had come, the supreme good, the Good of Goods. After lying so long hidden, all the manuscripts in the world, all the texts of Greek or Roman antiquity could have come to light suddenly at the beginning of the century, but without peace, riches, well-being, security, who would have dreamed of devoting himself to study?

Let us go further. Who profited from such peace and security? Certainly not the nobles, for at about this time they began the long and slow decline into poverty or lives as mere private citizens. As nobles they were not permitted to earn money. They neither wanted nor knew how to save what money they had. So they spent freely and found themselves in debt. Soon, if the king did not come to their aid with a lucrative office or position, or a pension of some sort, their lot would be poverty and loss of noble status.

The profits of the peace went to the man of the middle class. His was the rising class for many reasons, but above all because the modern state was taking shape bit by bit, with its specialized bureaucracy, basic services, and need for informed and technically trained people in law, administration, diplomacy, and finance. With rare exceptions, these people were not nobles. They were recruited from the middle class and from that part of the clergy that shared their values. These men, by their skilled and patient labor, made the modern state and its services function and prosper. They had money which they could lend to the king and which they knew how to manage. With this double strength, their future was assured.

The ticket to success was neither birth nor inherited wealth. Wealth did no harm, but it was not a prerequisite. In fact, among the men who rose to honor, there were people who had started with nothing and who became very rich. There have always been nouveaux riches, and there always will be, but they are not (as an idle people think of them) a useful butt for stand-up comics, the perfect scapegoat for general ill-will, or a phenomenon unknown before the First World War.

Not at all. Recent wealth is the daily bread of the historian, the spice of social history. No one has demonstrated this better than the great Belgian historian Henri Pirenne, in his book published in 1914—that is, before the war—on the *Stages in the Social History of Capitalism.*[8] He explains very clearly how, in the course of the history of capitalism, each period offered the businessman special conditions and special possibilities. Thus, the qualities which are useful to such men in one period may no longer be so (and are often detrimental) in the next period. It follows naturally that each change brings forth a new generation of newly rich. As time passes the nouveaux riches have old money, a new group of nouveaux riches appears, and the cycle begins again. In the sixteenth century, the man who started with nothing and aimed high, lacking birth and fortune, needed only one thing: knowledge.[9] Learning was the means and the tool for success, not just for a few individuals but for a whole social class which started at the bottom and aimed high.

II

The best means of fulfilling the new demand for learning was invented at just this time: printing. It is a commonplace to suggest that the invention of movable type was the "cause" of the Renaissance, by creating easy access to the great works of antiquity. I do not deny this view, but let us pay close attention to dates.

Printing, which began at a time when capitalism was beginning to be well organized, was from the very start a capitalist industry. I mean that the workers in the book business from the start worked for bosses who owned the necessary implements and had the necessary capital or were able to obtain it from silent

28

partners. Such capitalists and their partners were neither supermen ahead of their time nor disinterested philanthropists. Quite simply, they printed what there was the best market for, what would sell. The classics were not included. In the beginning, from 1480 to 1500 and a bit later, during the period of the first printers in France and their successors, what kind of demand would there have been in France for an edition of Greek tragedies or Latin speeches? When there were perhaps ten people in the kingdom who could read Greek, the demand for Plato in the original must have been slight.[10] (Furthermore, a Greek Plato had already been printed in Italy, so that someone who really wanted such a text could get it in Venice or Lyons.)

What was first made readily available and popularized by printing was not at all Renaissance literature, if we may use a crude but familiar system of classification, but the literature of the Middle Ages. This should be understood above all to mean religious books for the use of the clergy, missals and breviaries, collections of ready-made sermons, pious books for the faithful, and more than anything else, in edition after edition, Books of Hours, fiercely sought after by book collectors today, exquisite volumes, products of the early sixteenth century, with intricate borders, patterned bands, and fine woodcuts. Such Books of Hours served as family books, bedside books, often the only book in the house, the only book to be found where books were not read. They contained, in addition to prayers and the text of various church services, a calendar and an almanac. Sometimes the alphabet was included, to be used in teaching children to read; and on the fly-leaves the father generally kept track of marriages, births, and deaths in the family.

Schoolbooks, Donatus, Cato, *De Moribus in Mensa Servandis,* a whole collection of beginning Latin grammars, of elementary treatises on morals, simple and practical books spilled by the hundreds and thousands from the earliest presses.[11] In the same quantities royal ordinances poured forth, collections of edicts, texts of customs (the law codes of the day) to be used by judges and businessmen. By hundreds and thousands little popular pamphlets in French poured forth at low cost, making their way into the guard rooms of chateaux or the living rooms of merchants with no pretense of learning. There were stories about brave heroes or giants, collections of amusing anecdotes and jokes, almanacs and predictions, shepherds' calendars, recipes, and folk tales about Gargantua, Merlin the magician, or if intended for ladies, Amadis of Gaul.

The classics were printed as well. In Paris they appeared (as it happened) from the very start. But in general such books were published slowly, late, and prudently, only after a demand had been shown to exist. Printing did not create Renaissance customers; it merely served them once they existed. Printing's great achievement lay elsewhere.

In 1420 the man who wished to learn needed a teacher who could speak to him, who could dictate the lessons. The students sat at the foot of the master and wrote as he spoke. They wrote as fast as they could, introducing many mistakes and errors and deformations into these words seized on the fly. In this way they made their own books, for they had no others. Manuscripts were for the luxury trade, they were precious objects. The rarest were attached by a chain to the lectern on which they lay in the well-protected library of some prince or abbey or university. The chain may be taken as a symbol. Printing loosed the chain; that was its achievement. By 1500 the poor man who wanted to learn could, for a few pennies, provide himself with a grammar, a Greek or Hebrew dictionary, and all alone, in odd moments, in spare time, learn the most difficult languages, the most hermetic disciplines. Masters ensconced in their high wooden chairs were no longer needed. Printing created masters by the thousands, always ready to teach, anywhere, anyone, any time, a master which a person could himself possess and choose. That was the great change wrought by the new art of printing.

It was only then, when France enjoyed peace, and everyone hoped to rise in the world, and more and more print shops appeared, only then, between 1490 and 1520, that Humanism flourished. Then the thought of classical times began to reveal itself, and then, as radiant as a Florentine Primavera [spring], the Renaissance burst forth.[12]

It came at the right time. It is true that formalism reigned at the end of the fifteenth century, that art had become dry and sterile. People who for the first time in many a year could breathe freely and deeply, people who lived a broad and happy life, felt an unquenchable desire to grasp and apprehend life in all its forms, real life, not its shadow, not the fleshless skeleton of life reduced to a mummy. People turned away with distaste, with a kind of instinctive horror, from the teachings of death which were offered on all sides.[13] Suddenly antiquity was accessible, its concern for man, its cult of the individual, its knowledge of man in action, of man in contemplation, man living freely, letting one idea follow another, thinking clearly and boldly. It was an illumination. The best thinkers among them until then, exasperated by the vain

31

babble, had taken refuge, sought and found themselves in a secret and solitary mysticism. But in a hardworking world, in the world of the sixteenth century, bustling like a hive with activity, lively and ardent, mysticism had become a lost cause, a kind of suicide. The mechanical and sterile logic of the late scholastics taught in the schools was treated with derision or as a challenge. Man resolutely turned his back on the cell where the spirit of the *Imitation of Christ*[14] lived a solitary existence and, rolling up his sleeves like a manual laborer, he set to work. As for the nasty murderous little world of the sophists, Erasmus and Rabelais would take care of that. They buried it in ridicule. Next to the image of Gargantua made dull by his masters, stammering, dirty, shamefast, not knowing what to do but shift his cap in his hands and bellow like a calf, they placed the image of the centaur, the svelte image of the Renaissance, the harmonious body of Epistemon, pure and handsome as a young David, who, trained in the Humanist school of the classics, kept close to his heart at all times his self-awareness and the free use of his reason.[15]

Classical ideas and ideals suddenly became immensely attractive. Imagine, everything needed to be found, created, recreated, rediscovered. And people threw themselves passionately into the task. Think of the state of Greek studies in France. Neither grammars nor dictionaries nor texts nor teachers were to be found, or few of them—one or two adventurers who happened through and generally knew almost nothing of that which they claimed to teach.[16] Strong of heart and will, those who set to work did so with a determination to succeed. And those few were like Champollion bent over the Rosetta stone, intent on deciphering mysterious hieroglyphics.

III

What amazing careers these self-taught men had. The most remarkable perhaps is that of Thomas Platter of Basle, who, like his two sons, has left us an odd autobiography.[17] He was born a peasant of peasant stock in a poor village in the Valais.[18] His father died. His mother remarried. The rosary was unknotted and the beads dispersed, sons one way, daughters another, all the children went where chance took them. Thomas was the youngest. His father's sisters, pitying him, took him in. But once he was six he had to earn his own living. He became a servant, a poor little goat boy following his goats up the Alps, onto inaccessible rocks, across the forest and along precipices, barely escaping death twenty times. At nine and a half he was sent to school, placed in the hands of the local priest, with the hope that if he applied himself he too might one day become a priest. But school was the worst thing yet. School was the whip so brutally and freely used that the coarse peasants of the Valais themselves sometimes intervened. Worn out, the child ran away. At that moment one of his cousins passed through the town. At sixteen he was one of those nomadic students, called Followers of Bacchus, who lived by begging as they traveled along. But they did not extend their own hand for alms. They made use of wretched children, called *béjaunes,* to soften people's hearts and beg for bread, eggs, fruit. If need be these children would help themselves whenever an opportunity arose. So Thomas became a *béjaune,* a beggar, a thief, and a singer also, like the young Luther on the streets of Eisenach. He was led on an interminable odyssey from the Valais, to Lucerne, to Zurich, to Namburg, to Halle, to Dresden, to Breslau, to Nuremberg, to Munich . . . with occasional trips back to the Valais, followed by new departures. A life marked by short periods of happiness when some charitable soul took care of the poor child, and by long periods of misery when the little *béjaunes* refused to walk any further on their bleeding feet and were whipped on the calves by the pitiless Followers of Bacchus who drove the children on like cattle.

One day, when he was eighteen, Thomas Platter came to Sélestat. He could barely read. He went to the famous school of Johannes Sapidus. With a heroic effort he tried to clear the heavy layer of cobwebs from his brain. He carried on single combat with the Latin grammar of Donatus. Soon he was employed as a teacher, half tutor, half valet, to the two sons of a bourgeois family. During the day he served his masters. At night, he studied alone, fighting sleep by putting cold water or raw turnips or pebbles in his mouth to put his teeth on edge so that he would wake immediately should he doze off. In this way he taught himself Latin, Greek, and a bit of Hebrew. His entire fortune consisted of a single gold coin which he spent without regret on a Hebrew Bible to be devoured in silence. But he had to earn his living and the duties of a private tutor did not please him. In Basle he became a rope-maker. At about the same time and in the same place the great and courageous Sebastion Castellion, who proclaimed the coming reign of toleration to Calvin's face, was earning his living by pulling out of the river Birse the logs which the rushing current carried down from the mountains on days of high water. In his spare time, Castellion translated the Bible.[19]

Platter, under the direction of a coarse and brutal master rope-maker, learned the trade. At night, he rose secretly and lighted a sputtering candle. By its uncertain light, and with the help of a Latin trot, he learned to read Homer in Greek. In the morning, he returned to his ropes. The strange workman did not pass unnoticed in Basle. One day the poor manual worker, Platter, engaged in his trade at Saint Peter's Square where he was helping to make a thick rope, was stopped in his work by none other than Beatus Rhenanus, the great Alsatian Humanist. He too was a simple man, one of those open and hard-working good giants of the early Renaissance. And, on another day, at the same spot, another man could be seen, a shrunken little fellow, almost lost in his great coat, Mister Desiderius Erasmus in person, the greatest, the prince, the king of Humanists. Like Rhenanus, he too offered Platter a more comfortable way of earning his living, a position as tutor. Platter refused. Like Zwingli, to mention only one example, Platter had a touching respect for manual labor. A little later another strange scene took place in Basle. Oporinus, the great printer, had also come to Platter and had obtained from him the promise that each day for an hour Platter would teach him Hebrew. Platter came to keep his promise. But in the agreed-upon place he found not Oporinus alone, but twenty people, learned men, pastors, magistrates, doctors, and even a Frenchman rich enough to have a silk cape and his own servant.[20] The poor rope-maker was intimidated by this gathering and wanted to flee. Oporinus persuaded him to remain, to sit, to teach. And from then on, every evening he could be seen in that room, seated near the warmth of the pottery stove in his leather workman's apron, his hands covered with calluses and sometimes bloody from his work, with his coarse, unkempt, bearded peasant's face, doing his best to teach those who gathered to learn what he knew: Hebrew.

Nor was this a unique case. The times abounded in

men like that, wholly possessed by an epic thirst for learning. Toward 1471 we find Jean Standonck walking from Gouda to Paris (a distance of 400 miles) in the hope of getting a scholarship to one of those convents where the students suffered constantly from cold, dirt, and hunger. The canons regular of Sainte-Geneviève took him in as a servant. During the day he worked in the kitchen and at night he learned. As he was sometimes too poor to buy a candle, he found that if he climbed the bell tower at night he could read by the rays of the moon, gratis.[21] And in the same way later, Guillaume Postel, the great orientalist of mid-century, was a servant at the Collège de Navarre and taught himself Greek and Hebrew at night. Still later we find Peter Ramus the valet of a rich student who, likewise, spent his nights in study and prepared, one by one, all the examinations so that he became, finally, director of the Collège de Presles.

Strong men, as harsh toward others as they were toward themselves, such men understood little of pity or kindness or tenderness or "humanity." Standonck was the originator of the savage statutes of the Collège de Montaigu. The regime he established there was so severe that Rabelais, following Erasmus, declared it to be worse than the punishment dealt to criminals at forced labor by the Moors or the Tartars. "And if I were the king of Paris, may the devil take me if I wouldn't set fire to the college and burn it down, along with the principal and regents who permit such inhumanity to take place under their noses."[22] Platter, teaching his son Felix, of whom he was very proud and whom he loved as much as he was able, one day struck him with a rod across the eye so hard that he nearly lost the use of it. But neither severity nor brutality nor privations nor the terrible conditions which prevailed in the colleges discouraged children from studying.

Boys from comfortable homes were, in this respect, just like the magnificent and singular self-taught men of whom Platter is the prototype. Henry de Mesmes, at thirteen, studying at the Collège de Toulouse, got up every day at four, and having said his prayers, went to class at five, his books under one arm, a candle and lapboard under the other. Course followed course, from five until ten without a break. Then there was lunch, followed by recreational reading of Sophocles or Aristophanes or Euripides, perhaps a bit of Demosthenes, Cicero, Virgil, or Horace. At one, classes began again until five. The hour before dinner was spent going over the work of the day. At six there was dinner and another recreational reading period, reading Greek or Latin.[23] Such was the life of youth bereft of tenderness or special handling; such was the thirst for learning in a harsh age.

IV

There was an evident danger in all this. Recall the characteristics by which in the beginning we tried to define, in advance, someone in the sixteenth century studying literature: serious, hard-working, avid for book learning, and one might add, well served by an extraordinary memory. Might not such a person slip into a servile and literal adoration of all the ancients, minor as well as great, compilers as well as original thinkers? The danger is obvious; many critics and historians have spoken of it. They complain that the Renaissance, sent to study the ancients, wasted and despoiled the treasure trove of originality, of native French genius which had been formed during the

Middle Ages. Classical dogma was quite simply substituted for the old dogmas of yesteryear. Let me say straight off, and with all the more force since it is not always said: what saved them from this peril was their rusticity and their nomadic life.

For these people accustomed to the out-of-doors, for these "field crops," nature counted. They had lived, and often they continued voluntarily to live, in the country regardless of age or station. And like all rural people, they devoted a special kind of committed, almost unconscious attention to even the most minute details of nature about them. They did not respond to it aesthetically as far as we can tell. They did not all draw great philosophical truths from it, and their experience of nature did not necessarily tend toward the Rabelaisian myth of Physis, a Nature with broad fertile loins who gently cradles humanity in her arms until the day when, reassured and confident, they are lulled to sleep against the breast of our Good Mother the Earth. . . . But they all did have, from birth on, a committed and considered interest in plants, animals, trees. This should not lead us to believe that they were all perfect observers. Observation is difficult. Proper observation in the interests of science poses many obstacles even for us; how many more must there have been in the sixteenth century? Opening any book of the period, no matter who the author—with the possible exception of two or three great geniuses, and sometimes even then—we find monsters, apparitions, divine signs, or diabolic ones, predictions of the future, miracles. If the earth quakes, it is to announce the wrath of God. If the sun sets red behind a purple cloudbank, it is a sign of war and bloodshed to come. If a madman throws himself into an icy river and is pulled out in time, warmed and cared for so that he survives, it is a miracle due, no doubt, to the fact that he invoked the name of the Holy Virgin as he fell.

Today we carry about with us, from our first steps, the comfortable and practical conception of a determinist nature. The least philosophical parents teach this idea, all unawares, to even the dullest of their children as early as possible. We surround these children, from their infancy, with suggestions of solutions according to reason. We make every effort to dispel all those phantoms of yore, all the instinctive, foolish fears of children which their mothers' and grandmothers' tales carefully fostered in them. By comparison with the men of the sixteenth century, with the best minds of that epic period, the most credulous child of today is a model of critical sense.

Let us look at a physician who has, deservedly, the reputation of being an excellent doctor, Felix Platter, the son of that Thomas Platter whose early years were our subject a few pages ago. Felix studied medicine at Montpellier. When he was almost thirty and in his fourth or fifth year of medical studies, a servant was arrested one day and accused of having, three years earlier, killed his master, a canon. To convict the accused, the victim was disinterred and the supposed criminal was placed before the three-year-old cadaver. Platter, observing this scene, was greatly astonished to find that contrary to its duty, if one can put it that way, the corpse did not begin to bleed as soon as it was in the presence of its murderer. Felix writes: "Nonetheless none of the expected signs appeared, as, for example, the reopening of the wounds to pour forth fresh blood."[24] The impression he gives is of a certain degree of astonishment at the display of bad manners.[25]

The mind of man had to be washed clean of the accumulated layers of superstition, shaved clear of the beard of fantasy, before he could see; for it is with the brain, not with the eyes, that man sees. Two or three centuries more would be needed to complete the process. Let us nevertheless honor men who, by an enormous effort of self-control, wondrously ahead of their time, lifted themselves high enough to look the world and man in the face, straight in the face.

That is where the ancients were useful. It cannot be denied that much that was error, superstition, uncorroborated belief, was accepted as gospel under the aegis of their authority. But on the other hand, those same ancients provided the example of a skeptic like Lucian, a nonbeliever like Lucretius, above all, a philosopher like Cicero, the Cicero of the *De Natura Deorum* or the *De Divinatione,* or a man of learning like Pliny. The ancients were the teachers of rationalism for the sixteenth century.[26] And with this teaching they bound up the very wounds which they, or those like them, caused.

Moreover, the nomadic spirit of the times, when nothing seemed solidly anchored to the ground, when merchants spent their entire lives on the road, when students drifted from city to city, when courtiers followed the king from province to province—that nomadic spirit served another purpose. The people of the sixteenth century had not only a great thirst for knowledge but also a great hunger to see new things, to travel, to conquer space. They wanted to push back the limits of their ignorance, enlarge the lighted circle of human knowledge and human reason. Nor was this enough. These men, by means of their expeditions, both apprehensive and confident, wanted to push back the very limits of the world. New worlds were opening all over. The conquistadors, who were not all Spaniards, threw themselves into the search for worlds still

40

shrouded in mystery. Others were attracted by the Orient, the old Orient which had fascinated their fathers and their fathers' fathers before them. It would be interesting to make a catalogue of all the learned men, men of letters and study, who rushed to Venice, to the doorway of Islam, at the first possible chance, and thence to the Levant, Syria, the Nile.[27] Everything intrigued them, the vestiges of Hellenism, old manuscripts tucked away in convents, unknown plants, new animals. They saw men, too, with strange customs and strange religions. They faced the fascinating enigma of Islam and the Turk. And they went, despite the obstacles, the dangers, and the privations, drawing back at nothing. Sometimes they were captured by the Barbary pirates, sold as slaves, groaning for three or four years under the blows of a master until they were liberated, ransomed. Then, having by some miracle saved all their notes, they set vigorously to the task of putting them in order.[28]

They were consumed by a feverish desire to know, to understand, which encompassed not only the geographical and physical world but also that other world within man. In Montpellier around 1540 students went to the cemetery every night to steal freshly buried corpses, risking death twenty times over. They spent the night dissecting, trying to penetrate the secrets of the construction of the human body, revealed to the world by Vesalius.[29] As early as 1507, Copernicus began his study of the system of the world. It occupied him for twenty-three years (1507–1530), and when he had done, Copernicus, denying the old geocentric hypothesis, proclaimed, as Leonardo da Vinci had, that the earth was not at the center of the universe, nor the center of the sun's course. It was not only the earth which was pushed out of a usurped throne. By the same stroke, God too was forced to flee, so to speak, before man, and to seek refuge in the infinite spaces of the heavens.

V

That is what is needed to complete and correct the narrow and artificial view of the Renaissance which literary historians tend to give us. No one would challenge the fact that in the Renaissance, classical thought and learning were absorbed and assimilated as thoroughly as they could be by people separated from them by ten centuries, people whose hearts and brains had been formed by ten centuries of Christianity. The Renaissance brought those ideas, but it did other things as well.

The mobility of the early sixteenth century; the anxiety of sorts which pushed man ever onwards, following the road further and further; their sense of country life, of the rhythms of nature; their peasant endurance; their detachment from those things which have most hold on us today, the hearth, the family, love itself; in short, their toughness, their native peasant qualities which must have been present as well in the Crusaders or in the Mendicants, the early Franciscans of the thirteenth and fourteenth centuries who founded monasteries and bishoprics in the heart of Asia[30]—these are the things which must be put in one pan of the balance scale while the other holds the scholarly strengths and merits of the people of those times.

Such men could not have been slaves to antiquity. When Gargantua, with his enormous, symbolic appetite, sits at the table, all nature lies richly spread before him, including antiquity. As he sits, he makes the sign of the cross, saying grace like a Christian. Classical thought, Christian tradition, cult of nature, at one and the same time, that is what those men of violent passions nourished, or more properly, gorged themselves with. They devoured it all mixed up together. To digest and assimilate all that they stuffed themselves with in a few decades would be the work of two centuries, for what was the seventeenth century if not the hundred-year-long digestion, the slow assimilation of all the contradictory and diverse ideas that the sixteenth century swallowed? Rabelais was not wrong to make Gargantua and Pantagruel giants. He was merely giving his age its due.

3

The Quest for Beauty

Renaissance: the word is impressive, evocative, and yet imprecise. It has two meanings: it may refer to an intellectual phenomenon or to an aesthetic one. The relation between them was once thought easy to explain. In this view Charles VIII brought back both the literary and the artistic Renaissance in the supply wagons which returned from Fornovo. France and Italy at the end of the fifteenth century offered a strong contrast: the decadence of the gothic in France; radiant quattrocento Italy, aglow with the achievements of her painters and sculptors. Clearly, our forefathers, presented with the incredible abundance of masterpieces to be found in the smallest Italian towns, must have been dazzled, overwhelmed, contrite. They must immediately have beat their breasts, recognizing their own aesthetic ignorance, and they would have begun at once to repair so regrettable a neglect. And in fact, from the first years of the new century chateaux sprang up along the Loire as if by magic. Bit by bit classical decoration replaced gothic motifs; while François I brought Italians to France, men such as Leonardo da Vinci, Benvenuto Cellini, and Prima-ticcio.[1] Soon, built on the ruins of the old gothic, the new classical art could be seen in the Palace of the

44

Louvre, the Tuileries, a hint of the logical magnificence and rational splendors of the seventeenth century.

Not everyone accepted this view of the Renaissance. There were those who felt that it was one-sided, that Italian influence was not so vital as was generally claimed. But they agreed to argue on their adversaries' own ground. There were others who burst with indignation at the Italian triumphs, and burned with grief and despair that imported culture should have crushed the genius of France. They cursed the Renaissance as the death knell of true French art.

Of late we have got beyond such discussions. Efforts have been directed, first of all, toward precise and detailed investigations of men and things: the Italians who came to France at the start of the sixteenth century; the works of art produced in France at the same time. There have been objective attempts to discover what the great architecture and great painting of the period owes to Italy and what it owes to native traditions. All this is legitimate, reasonable, and useful. But it is beyond the limits of our concerns here, and, from our point of view, not very satisfying.

The fundamental error in all such research is the assumption that in France on the eve of the Italian wars, at the end of the fifteenth and the beginning of the sixteenth centuries, there was such a thing as indigenous French art, distinct from any other, strictly national, owing nothing to anyone. By art in this context is meant, of course, the whole gamut of arts, so that we must imagine an architecture properly called French architecture, along with sculpture, painting, and printmaking, equally French.

The old theory has it that quite suddenly the Alps were no longer a barrier; Italians rushed to France.

Indigenous art, national art, strictly and narrowly French, suddenly was transformed and then supplanted by an imported art. If we look beyond architecture at the evidence presented by other arts— sculpture, painting, miniatures, engraving—it becomes obvious that in the France of the end of the reign of Louis XI or of Charles VIII, there was no such thing as French art in the sense in which we might want to use the term today. In France during that period were artistic centers where artists produced cosmopolitan art, European art, the art of the North.[2] Or, if you prefer, the situation can be seen as a rivalry, in the fifteenth and sixteenth centuries, of the Flemings and the Italians. Each brought their artistic wealth to France, placed midway between them, land of the golden mean, land of mingling and conciliation. One of the two combatants had to win, either Italy or Flanders. For the fifteenth century there can be no doubt that the North was champion. So great was the Flemish victory that Flemings crossed the mountains and rallied the very Italians to their banner in the midst of the triumphant and magnificent quattrocento. Was it not an Italian, Bartolomeo Facio, who in 1465, in his *De Viris Illustribus,* proclaimed Jan van Eyck the greatest painter in the world? May we not take as symbolic the old story that Antonello da Messina came to Flanders to learn the secrets of painting in oil?[3] Roger van der Weyden traveled to Italy around 1450. The number of important works commissioned by Italians from this northern master and painted by him in Italy attests to the position Flemish painting had won for itself across the Alps.

Suddenly, at the start of the sixteenth century, there was a rapid, total, and decisive change. Italian art turned, faced the enemy, and attacked in turn. It took the offensive with stunning speed. In a few short years it had conquered, enslaved, and crushed Flanders and Germany. Few changes in the history of the arts are so sudden and so total.

This was the clash which took place over French soil. The French were by no means disinterested observers of the vicissitudes of the conflict. To treat it abstractly, imagining a purely Italian indigenous art opposed by an equally pure and equally indigenous French national art, each nation completely closed to the other until the barrier between them was breached by the lucky stroke of war, the victor vanquished by the arts of the conquered people, Graecia capta . . . , is an oversimplification. ["Captive Greece took her fierce victor captive and brought the arts into rustic Latium" (Horace, *Epistles,* II, ll. 156–157).] No understanding of the question is possible from such a point of view. To espouse it is to embrace in advance the gravest of errors and misunderstandings.

I

Before we investigate the state of French art on the eve of the Renaissance, let us be quite clear what is meant by French art. Within the borders of what is France today there were a number of artistic centers associated with the courts of rich, generous, and cultivated noblemen, patrons of a type which became more frequent as the fourteenth century yielded to the fifteenth: Jean de Berry, René de Provence, Philip the Good, to name only a few.[4] Such centers represented nothing national in the modern sense of the word. And it should be remembered that the borders of France in the fifteenth century, in 1475, say, just before the death of Charles the Bold, last Duke of Burgundy, were not at all those we know today. This too presents innumerable and insurmountable difficulties in defining a national style. Was Picardy French? Probably, but it belonged to the Duke of Burgundy. And Artois and Arras? They too were Burgundian. But Charles the Bold, after all, was a French noble,[5] and, as for Artois, it was a fief of the king of France, or at least it was until the treaty of Madrid (1526) confirmed by the treaty of Cambrai (August 3, 1529). For the next century it was to be out of French control. And Lille? Saint-Omer? Bruges? Ghent? They were all Burgundian cities, recognizing Charles the Bold as their sovereign. We can perhaps include as French Lille and Saint-Omer, but not Bruges or Ghent. But by what rational means is this separation to be made? All four are Flemish cities, in exactly the same political position with respect to France. Looking at maps of the Kingdom of France in 1476, 1610, and 1648, we find that for a century and a half Arras, Cambrai, Lille, Ypres, Bruges, Ghent, all equally were out of France, governed by enemies of the king of France. And the same question can be asked for Lorraine, Burgundy, the Franche-Comté, Savoy; and answering it presents the same problems. Obviously the projection of the present, which has no special claim to eternity, into the past is not acceptable. The difficulty lies in the question itself. The modern definition of nations does not apply. And in the same way, the spirit of the art of the time was not "national."

The thought and the arts of the Middle Ages were thoroughly international. In the thirteenth and fourteenth centuries all civilized Europe shared a common Christian civilization. The internationalism of thought, science, and art, served by a common international language, Latin, was still a force in the fifteenth century. And it continued to exist in spite of the rise of nations. The artists who gathered in the artistic centers mentioned earlier were not necessarily or even usually natives of the country in which they worked. They were nomads. They came from everywhere. The Burgundian school of sculpture, centered in Dijon, was founded by a Hollander, Claus Sluter,[6] or at least it was he who spread its fame. It flourished thanks to artists not one of whom was a native of Burgundy. The Cologne school of painting, which can be studied there at the Wallraf Museum and which seems so coherent, homogenous, and unified, does not have a single native of Cologne among its major painters. There were Swabians like Stephan Lochner,[7] Antwerpers like Joos van Cleve, the Master of the Death of Mary, Hollanders like Barthelemy Bruyn, and even, at the end, a Frenchman, Pierre des Mares. The school of Avignon[8] is made up of men from Picardy, Burgundy, the Limousin, the Ardeche, and even Catalonia. None from Avignon. Painters came from all over, like the Humanists who also came from everywhere and went anywhere. To what country did Erasmus belong? Can he really be limited to the County of Holland? Artists became attached, not to a nation, but to a master, a master who had been their master in all senses of the word, who had taught them their craft, passed on his secret mixtures, his habits, his techniques. What determined their style was, on the one hand, the lessons of this master, piously followed, and on the other, the particular artistic tastes of the patrons for whom they worked, who often had very distinct aesthetic ideas which they imposed absolutely upon the artists working for them.

These preliminary remarks should make clear how wrong it is to speak of a French art of the fifteenth century as though we meant a style which was deeply national, homogeneous, coherent, easy to identify, or with clearly fixed limits. There is a document which is vital to any examination of the evolution of art in this part of the world in the fourteenth and fifteenth centuries: that marvel of marvels, that jewel of the collection gathered at Chantilly by the Duc d'Aumale, the *Très Riches Heures* of the Duc de Berry. Anyone turning the pages of this volume or of a reproduction will be struck with wonder by its beauty, and then, a moment of bewilderment follows. To what school should these glorious miniatures be attributed? The Flemish? Yes and no. There is, at certain points, a Flemish atmosphere of sorts, but, examined more closely, the miniatures lack, for example, the fabric folds which are so perfectly characteristic of all the products of the Flemish school at this period. The work is certainly not Italian, although it is filled with details reminiscent of the Italian style, not to mention the pages which reproduce entire Italian paintings. (For example, Taddeo Gaddi's *Presentation of the Virgin at the Temple,* which is in Santa Croce in Florence, is quite precisely reproduced in one of these miniatures.) And no one who knows the work of the Siennese school of the trecento, soft, charming, and emotive, can fail to see its reflections in the Chantilly manuscript. In other pages there are recollections or borrowings from the Orient, others which owe a debt to classical antiquity, familiar classical groups reproduced or cleverly used by the painters working for Jean de Berry. Or again, there are old medals brought to life or oriental miniatures which seem to be the inspiration behind certain crucial pages. The whole is held together by a great sense of life, of intimacy, and of the French countryside, especially in the wonderful pages of the Calendar.[9]

International art is perhaps too grand a name. It was

art intended for the use and the taste of Jean, Duke of Berry, executed by some of the best practitioners of the day. Jean, a French prince and French in his tastes, was the most alert and broad-ranging of art lovers, and his field of interest extended without clear limits to all that which was beautiful and new.

Perhaps we should ask whether by their very beauty, their noble origin, their aesthetic merit, the *Très Riches Heures* are not a unique document, one of those masterpieces to which the usual rules do not apply, masterpieces which should not be stressed as part of a study of the normal development of the arts. There is truth in this, but it is also true that the influences which blend so harmoniously there can be found, glimpsed, seen everywhere during the whole of the fifteenth century in all the works of art commissioned by French princes, cities, or groups on what is today French soil. Obviously it is not always so wisely handled, so well done, and so generally successful. The combinations were varied to suit the patrons and to suit the painters as well. Moreover, the less skillful they are, the easier it becomes to analyze them and separate them into component parts from diverse provinces.

II

In his excellent book, whose central thesis I am unable to accept as it stands but which nonetheless is thorough, Emile Mâle addresses some of the major questions posed by this art.[10] What spirit did it reflect? What needs did it fulfill? What feelings did it reveal? Whereas in the thirteenth century Christian art is regular, even, and serious, with an unbroken and unequaled serenity, at the end of the fourteenth and by the fifteenth centuries a new iconography appeared, changing the character of the arts.[11] They became picturesque, pathetic, human. The picturesque is an important innovation. Nothing could be more foreign to the arts of the thirteenth century than this interest in anecdote, in local color, in historical or pseudohistorical settings. Then all contingencies could be dealt with in terms of eternal images belonging to all time and all places: the fine God [le Beau Dieu] of Amiens, the Saint Theodore of Chartres, the Saint Stephen of Sens.[12]

But the art of the fifteenth century sought out the picturesque and individuating detail, for example, the costume of the time, of that time, of a social class or corporation. Saint Michael in the great doorway of Bourges [thirteenth century] weighs souls in a long robe with classic folds. Saint Michael in Dijon, in the altarpiece of Jacques de Baerze, is a fifteenth-century knight armed from head to toe; the precision with which his armor is depicted has been the delight of archeologists. God himself, God the Father who in the thirteenth century was hardly shown, as though artists hesitated before the idea of such majesty, became a frequent figure in the fifteenth century, a kind of royal Nestor, a bearded Charlemagne seated in glory, glove in hand like an emperor, tiara on his head like a pope. A naive distinction is made though; the pope's tiara has three crowns, God's has four or five.

Places, like costumes, became specific. The Annunciation of the thirteenth century takes place in a world of faith and hope. Both the Virgin and the angel stand draped in long robes while the divine message is received. By the fifteenth century, the Virgin is a young lady in a pretty blue dress who greets the angel in her oratory or in her bedroom, a room which is rendered down to the last bit of furniture, the last drapery. The

Brussels museum has a panel attributed to the Master of Flémalle in which one can even see, hanging on the wall, although somewhat before its time, an image of Saint Christopher bearing the Christ Child on his shoulder.[13] The setting has come down to earth from the heavens, to French earth, or Flemish, or German; we can tell where and almost in what year the scene is set.

Art ceased to be loftily impassive. The Christ triumphant of the thirteenth century yields to the suffering, tortured, crucified Christ of the fifteenth. The art of the fifteenth century took pleasure in following, slowly, from station to station, the stages of the Passion to the final moment in Golgotha without sparing us a wound, a fall, or a tear. The Passion, the cross of Christ, is continued in the cross of his tormented mother, more poignant still. The pietà became a favorite theme, the body of Christ, bleeding and helpless, resting on the lap of the heartbroken Virgin. In this way, through the taste for the picturesque and through the power of compression which it implies, art became more human, closer to the heart of man. It descended from its high pedestal to console, warm, encourage God's creatures. There is no use in developing these ideas further since they have been so skillfully presented by Emile Mâle.

Mâle attributes all these new characteristics of fifteenth century art to the mystery plays which began at just that time to be performed for enthusiastic crowds in village squares, in the streets, in front of cathedrals. The idea of connecting the art with the mystery plays is ingenious, and very appealing. It is also, I must remark in passing, insufficient. It fails to answer the question. Why does art become picturesque, emotional, and human? Because of the mysteries. But why

are the mysteries at just this time themselves picturesque, emotional, and human? Because of the influence of the *Meditations on the Life of Christ,* a little book
of Franciscan piety written in the thirteenth century,
once misattributed to Saint Bonaventure. And why
should the *Meditations* suddenly become popular, especially in France, two centuries after they were
written? To offer explanations of movements in art by
invoking the theater, and then to explain the theater
by reference to the *Meditations* is, even if the explanations are quite complete, only to put off the problem.
Why did taste change at just that moment? Why does
the art of the time take such satisfaction in the picturesque, the pathetic, and the human? The only possible
explanation, and it is one which Mâle does not give, is
of a change in the social order. At the very time we
find this change in art, society saw the rise of a new social class, original, active, inquiring, profoundly realistic in its tastes and its tendencies, making an ever
larger and better place for itself. This new class, the
bourgeoisie, which did not have any effect on the art of
the thirteenth century, influenced that of the fifteenth. At the end of the fourteenth century and the
start of the fifteenth, three changes took place: the rise
of the bourgeoisie; the spread over all Europe of a real-
ist art, practiced largely by middle-class Flemish
painters; the appearance of a new kind of subject
matter, bringing into paintings the themes of the picturesque, pathetic, and human. Did these three
changes come at the same time by chance, or were they
not rather mutually created?

III

The general evolution of the arts in countries like
France from the middle of the fifteenth century to the

first quarter of the sixteenth shows no sudden change corresponding to the change we saw at the end of the fourteenth either in art or in society. The art of the reign of Charles VIII and Louis XII was a continuation of that which pleased our forefathers under Louis XI or even Charles VII, or VI, or V. The same words come to mind to describe it. There are no great works, but many charming minor ones to be found all over, in churches, old manors, little rustic roadside chapels, on the front of middle-class town houses. The period produced many stained-glass windows, glowing with color and rich with pattern, whose general subject matter and style were no different from that of the other art forms of the period. And there was the multitude of miniatures, at once picturesque and human. Bit by bit, from the beginning to the end of the century, a kind of relaxation and broadening took place. But changes which distinguish later works from earlier ones are so gradual as to be nearly imperceptible. If we follow a single homogenous school with marked characteristics, the Burgundian, for example, throughout the fifteenth century, it produced fundamentally the same art, as picturesque, pathetic, and human as one might wish. The greatest difference to be found in the works at the very end of the period, giving life to the somewhat stiff bodies depicted earlier, is a kind of joy which started to appear on the faces, earlier closed and sad or expressionless. But there is no need to suggest that this change comes from Italy when we can look to peace, the simple pleasures of everyday life, and the natural progress of an art which would develop greater scope and control of its own idiom with time.

Let the experts say what they please. Let them develop the mechanical abstraction of genres generating genres, forms generating forms. I shall bow respectfully to their knowledge and admire the precision with which their research is documented, but I shall not concede this one point: when a society does not change, people do not change. When a society undergoes no sudden mutations but only slow evolution, no new style can take hold either through fashion or fad. No matter how high one's credit stands with that society, one cannot impose upon it an art which does not respond fully to its needs. In this case, the art of the Italian quattrocento could not be forced on the France of Charles VIII and Louis XII.

What would the France of that period have done with the art of the quattrocento? It was not even a portable art. The painters of the period executed their greatest masterpieces in fresco which, by its nature, cannot be moved. In the course of the century the Italians became more interested in panel painting, which had long been a monopoly of the North. But their most successful efforts were still huge decorative frescos. How many first-rate Italian artists cannot be known by those who have not traveled in Italy, despite the fact that there are museums everywhere. Think of Giotto and his followers, of Masaccio in the Brancacci chapel in Florence. Signorelli, Ghirlandaio, Mantegna, even Raphael cannot be known without having seen their frescos.

But leaving this problem aside, there are others. The art of the various Italian schools was certainly not homogeneous, as the very fact that we speak of Italian schools in the plural testifies. However, despite the diversity of local or individual temperaments, from school to school, from master to master, certain characteristics are common to all those works and those men, characteristics which we see and feel as Italian without doubt or hestitation. Surely they were Italian enough so that it would have been impossible for those who bore such traits, just because they bore them, to exercise a serious and lasting influence on a land across the barrier formed by the Alps, whose customs were different from their own.

One of the most striking sights of Florence is, I believe, that which confronts the visitor to the Uffizi finding himself suddenly in front of Hugo van der Goes's great masterpiece, painted in about 1476 for Thomas Portinari, the Medici agent in Bruges. The visitor comes upon this painting after having gone through the rooms filled with Italian masterpieces of the quattrocento. Leaving the high galleries from which one can see as far as the wooded flanks of San Miniato, the visitor has his head filled with the lovely visions, harmonious compositions, and elegant figures of the Florentine school. He has lingered long over the subtle art of these *tondi,* each of which poses and solves with astonishing ingenuity a new problem of composition, of the management of line and form.

Then suddenly there is a huge panel.[14] Its bright and rich color commands attention. Its breadth of conception and execution impresses. Its strength is asserted with the simplicity born of self-assurance. What a contrast! There is nothing learned, ingenious, rare, subtly arranged. If one analyzes the composition, it seems almost awkward; the figures are out of scale, the foreground mismatched and somewhat bare. Yet what a sense of contemplation is conveyed by this large surface every part of which joins to create an atmosphere, even what at first seems to be clumsiness, even the ugliness of the graceless northern angels with their bony and pensive faces.

The contrast is violent; the conclusion is clear:

Flemings and Italians did not really speak the same language. Nor was the distinction recent. And what is true of Flemings and Italians, who represent the two extremes, was also true of Frenchmen and Italians. The French were arbitrators between the two rival centers of art in this case as in many others. They were not unfamiliar with the art of the other side of the Alps. We must not forget that they traveled a great deal. Rich men, princes and nobles, the men who commissioned the works, traveled and their travels developed in those of them who were so inclined a liberal and enlightened eclecticism. The artists too traveled. When Jean Fouquet of Tours, the very type of the painter in the reign of Louis XI, set up his studio in Paris first and later in Tours, he had already been to Italy from 1443 to 1447 and had already painted the portrait of Pope Eugene IV in Rome that Vasari mentions a century later.[15]

While the art of the North had no secrets for French artists, they clearly felt a need to temper, moderate, and modify it, introducing their own native qualities, a sly good humor, and a fine sense of proportion. But for them as for the Flemings, religious feelings were expressed not by noise, movement, light, or breadth of spectacle, but rather by silence and contemplation. For them no more than for the masters or the bourgeois of the North could the Nativity be set in a Florentine palace, as a social call to the mother of a newborn child by patrician Florentine ladies, dressed in brocades and silk embroidered with gold, seeking to please while at the same time, conscious of their rank, knowing how to walk before an admiring crowd of common people. In 1485, scarcely ten years after Hugo van der Goes had painted his great triptych, Ghirlandaio decided to paint an Adoration of the Shepherds for the Sassetti

chapel of the church of the Holy Trinity.[16] In it he
placed three peasants, depicted with great realism,
their brows marked with creases, their cheeks ill-
shaven, a clear indication of the influence which the
lifelike group of shepherds in the Portinari altarpiece
had on Florentine painting. In this charming work the
Florentine painter has neatly succeeded in linking the
three episodes, the Annunciation to the Shepherds,
the Adoration of the Shepherds, and the arrival of the
three Magi. Yet there is no sign of the quality which
truly distinguishes the unique value and charm of the
van der Goes painting. We see the pretty Virgin
kneeling before her son, elegant in her dress and
manners, with her sleek patrician hands, held softly
together so that we may admire them; the three shepherds who so kindly take their position in a corner of
the painting, one of them standing in the ritual posture of a theatrical mime who, one hand held over his
heart and the other extended before him, expresses
the faithful imitation of emotion. The Holy Infant
himself, in marked contrast with the wretched and
pathetic newborn child depicted by the Flemish
master, is a fat and rosy baby on the day of his birth,
already round and smiling like a ten-month-old. These
nice people, playing their parts in a drama from which
all expression of true piety has been banished by their
very appearance and postures, shut out the kind of
emotion which we have just referred to as contemplation, an emotion which is not very Italian but typical
of the North.

There is a significant detail in the work of the Florentine master: Saint Joseph, kneeling like the others
next to the two traditional animals, takes no part in
the Adoration. His eyes are not directed toward the
Christ Child, like those of the Virgin and the shep-

herds. Turning his fine and vacant gaze toward the landscape of the background, this nobleman seems, by look and gesture, to call the Magi, who in fact are coming toward the scene of the Adoration sumptuously dressed on their chargers, followed by a brilliant and varied crew. The faster they arrive the faster the movement, color, and spectacle will enter the silent, peaceful, and still scene of the Adoration which can be borne just long enough to make a quick sketch, but no longer, by these lively Italians.

The art of the quattrocento, while it lacks the sincere and deep, contemplative emotion of the North, has, on the other hand, an undeniable sense of the theatrical, or rather, the pathetic. It is not very sensitive to the intimate but it excelled from the first in depicting, in bringing forth, in bringing to life with a singular pathetic intensity, the great tragic scenes of classical and Christian antiquity. Think of the dramatic force of Giotto's frescos in the Arena chapel in Padua, or the upper church at Assisi. Even the choice of subjects—or more exactly, the way in which the subjects are portrayed, the moment in the story which is chosen by the Italians—merits closer attention.

In a judicious and suggestive book, a collection of comparative studies of *L'Art au nord et au sud des Alpes à l'époque de la Renaissance* [Art North and South of the Alps during the Renaissance] (Brussels, 1911), Jacques Mesnil quite rightly noted that when Flemings and Italians were faced with the task of dealing with so common a subject as the Last Supper, they went about it in totally different ways. The Last Supper as it is recorded in the Gospels consists of two scenes, according to Mesnil: Christ giving the apostles communion, and Christ speaking the terrible sentence, "Truly I say unto you, one of you shall betray me" (John 23:21). It is interesting to note that, quite naturally, and with fine intuition of the character of their talents, the Flemings tended to portray the interiorized drama of the communion. And they were enormously successful, as is proved, among other examples, in the *Last Supper* by Dirk Bouts in Saint Peter's at Louvain. Just as naturally, with the same sureness of instinct, the Italian masters tried to make manifest, to reproduce with all its emotional force, the scene of anguish, of stupefaction and indignant protestation which greeted Christ's words to the apostles. And they too succeeded perfectly in attaining their aims, as is attested by the devoted pilgrimages still made today to a certain wall of the refectory of Santa Maria delle Grazie in Milan where the fading outlines of Leonardo's *Last Supper* can still be made out.[17]

Doubtless Mesnil oversimplifies somewhat, for in fact there are not two but three distinct ways in which the Last Supper can be conceived and represented, and all three are frequently shown. The first is Christ breaking the bread (the Eucharist), the second the communion of the apostles, and the last, the dramatic scene of the revelation of the approaching betrayal. In fact it seems that this last scene may have been painted for the first time as late as 1480 by Ghirlandaio in his fresco for the Ognissanti refectory in Florence, only fifteen or so years before Leonardo captured that tragic moment for us in Milan. In the early fifteenth century Andrea del Castagno painted his famous fresco of the introduction of the Eucharist; he was followed by many painters of the quattrocento. Fra Angelico, in the convent of San Marco, chose to portray the communion given to the apostles. This scene was still being painted in 1512 in the cathedral of Cortona by Luca Signorelli (although in this case the major influence was a famous work by Joos van Ghent, painted around 1475 in Urbino by the Flemish master, commissioned by the confraternity of the Corpus Domini with the aid of the Duke, Federigo da Montefeltro).

The truth, it would seem, is more varied and subtle than Mesnil would have it. He is nonetheless right to suggest the contrast between the tendencies of the painters of the north to be most successful at depicting tender and intimate scenes and the tendencies of the Italians to excel at more dramatic ones. Contemporaries in the sixteenth century did not deny that such a division existed. Proof of this can be found, for example, in the *Four Talks on Painting,* lectures given in Rome in 1538–39 and collected (or written) in 1548 by Francisco da Hollanda, published by Joachim de Vasconcellos. The author puts these words about art into the mouth of Michelangelo: "Flemish painting will generally be more pleasing to the very pious than Italian painting which will never draw a tear, while the other will call forth floods. The cause of this lies not in the strength or the excellence of the painting, but in the goodness of the pious observer."[18]

It should also be noted that Italian artists, without a doubt, used a style that was too free, too casual about precise detail and fine finish that was characteristically Flemish to please the art lovers of the North. We must remember that what the bourgeois sees in a work of art is an imitation. The Italian masters of the fifteenth century did not excel in rendering draperies, rich cloth, and armor in imitation so accurate as to deceive the eye. Their art was by no means the art of the portrait, in the bourgeois sense of the word, and the Italians themselves were the first to admit it. In fact, they went further; when they wanted a precise image of themselves in a portrait, they sought out a Flemish master.[19] Think of how many portraits of Italians painted by northern masters are in museums today. Taking the work of van Eyck alone, there are the portraits of Arnolfini in London, Giustiniani in Dresden, Albergati in Vienna, and how many others? Later, when Masaccio, Paulo Uccello, Andrea del Castagno, Domenico Veneziano, and Fra Filippo Lippi were dead, when Andrea del Verocchio, the Pollaiuoli, Baldovinetti, and Mantegna were at the height of their powers, and Botticelli and Ghirlandaio at the start of their careers, one of the greatest collectors of the day, Federigo da Montefeltro, Duke of Urbino, wanting a series of portraits, called upon an artist from the North, Joos van Ghent. The taste of great connoisseurs and that of the bourgeois sometimes coincided. For the latter, the Flemings were the unequaled virtuosi of imitation. The works of the Flemish masters invited examination with a magnifying glass. Here was the wherewithal to please the naive crowd, who, incidentally, even today in the cathedral of Saint Bavo in Ghent, delight in using a large magnifying glass to count the hairs on the horses of the magistrates or the eyebrows of the patriarchs. Looking at the exquisite little panels, for example, in Bruges, in the calm of the Hospice of Saint John, we can imagine the pleasure with which they were received by those who commissioned them, how they were taken to a window so that they might catch the fullest light, drawing exclamations of joy when the happy owners discovered under magnification some previously unnoticed detail, the weave of some fabric perfectly imitated or the highlight of a jewel trapping the reflection of a leaded window.[20] At the moment when the last holds were being freed, when the middle class was coming fully into its own, one can understand that the men of the North, of Flanders, of Germany, and of France as well, might have preferred, as a matter of taste, the Flemish to the Italian. There is no mystery in this, or if there is, certainly not a mystery which cannot be easily explained.

IV

What remains to be explained is the sudden and major change described earlier. Italian art, limited to the Italian peninsula by the victory, so to speak, of the Flemish manner during the whole of the fifteenth century, suddenly broke free and spread beyond its traditional limits, taking pride of place, especially in Germany and the low countries. Why this great and total revolution?

I personally see a general cause. The world became learned at the end of the fifteenth century and the beginning of the sixteenth. People studied the Greco-Latin classics and found many fine ideas that would not have occurred to them before. Among them was the idea that the painter, always considered an artisan, included in the same corporation as saddlers and binders, a manual worker, a "mechanic," was in fact something other than an obscure and useful artisan. If he had talent, if he could reproduce life with his brush, breathe life into the past, dressing it in the vivid colors of the present, then he was one of the great men of this world, in his own eyes and in the eyes of men of arts and letters, the equal in nobility to princes and kings.[21] Well might Charles V, the emperor, stoop to pick up Titian's fallen brush. Much earlier Albrecht Dürer left the splendid city of Venice to return to his bourgeois Germany and remarked in heartfelt tones

these words rich in meaning: "In Venice I am a gentleman. In Nuremberg I am only a poor devil."[22]

The world became learned. People were guided by
the Greeks and the Romans. The world, Italy first of
all, well before the other countries of Europe, learned
from the classics not only about the outstanding dignity of art but also what art is: that it is Beauty. It
learned from Plato before learning it in Rome among
the cardinals' vineyards where classical statues were
gradually being rediscovered. It learned from Vitruvius who was read and glossed even before the
great Roman ruins strewn over Roman, Italian, or
Gaulish soil were understood, admired, or restored.
Rabelais' taste for books about architecture is quite
typical. He accepted them whether they were about
contemporary chateaux being built in Touraine or
Poitou—those which inspired his description of the
abbey of Theleme, based faithfully on the chateau of
Bonnivet—or about Roman ruins, of which, at the
time of his trip to Rome in 1534, he planned to give a
summary account.[23] By knowledge, by erudition, by at-
tentive study of Vitruvius and Alberti (inspired by
Vitruvius),[24] by contacts with the learned Philandrier[25]
(who wrote a commentary on Vitruvius), or with the
architect Philibert de L'Orme (whom he met in 1536
in Rome), Rabelais, whose great mind seems not to
have been especially responsive to the arts, came like
his century to be actively interested in that which was
for preceding ages, bricklaying, and which in his own
day would become architecture.[26]

At the same time that they turned to the classics,
the people of the sixteenth century turned to nature as
well and learned to observe. Art in Italy at the end of
the fifteenth century tended to become a science, or

more exactly, to rely on the precise rules of perspective and anatomy. The results of this movement can be seen in the magnificent, inspired work of a Leonardo, a learned and independent innovator as much as a fine painter. The whole of the quattrocento around him and before him had worked feverishly to conquer two things: a sure and scientific theory of perspective and a knowledge of human anatomy.[27] This was a specifically Italian effort, the like of which was not to be found in France or Flanders or Germany. By the end of the fifteenth century or the start of the sixteenth, the Italian artists were clearly the superiors of the Flemings with respect to composition, knowledge of anatomy, and perspective. The dead Christ painted by Mantegna, for example, moves us by the power of the foreshortening, at once bold and sure.[28] The Italian superiority was such, so strong and so clear, that no one could either question it or remain insensible of its attraction—or at least, no one who understood that art was, necessarily, in part science, no one whose eyes had been opened to the light of antiquity. Now it is clear why Italian art during the entire first half of the quattrocento had no influence in the North, why it did not spread beyond the limits of the Italian peninsula. The times were not yet ripe. For one thing, Italy was not yet master of its impressive technique; it was still being sought. Day by day the difficult science of perspective was being conquered, a precise knowledge of anatomy was being gained. At the time of the first signs of success, the men on the other side of the Alps were not yet ready to be interested by such things. Their natural taste for the art of northern painters, minute, precise, bright, and ungainly, remained whole and unquestioned. More time was needed, much more. Progress was needed first in Italian artistic technique, and also in northern intellectual culture, preparing the moment when, suddenly, the superiority of Italian art over the traditional art of the northern painters they had always preferred appeared with blinding clarity, as unquestionable as dogma.

The case should not be overstated. What Italian art controlled, dominated, and eliminated was the Flemish and German art of the sixteenth century, rather than the Flemish art of the fifteenth century, dear to the French. From Italy France took those things whose existence was not even suspected there before the sixteenth century: large canvases, paintings of mythological scenes, the huge pagan nudes of the Gallery of Fontainebleau.[29] These borrowings were quite natural; François I could not have turned to a Frenchman, a German, or a Fleming to produce the kind of works he desired, the works which were produced for him on the banks of the Loire by Gian Battisto Rosso in 1531, and beginning the next year, by Francesco Primaticcio of Bologna.

Architecture does not show quite the same pattern.[30] The chateaux along the Loire, those which we still visit and admire today, are not the work of Italians, despite their easily recognizable Italian elements. France produced a style at once composite and original, a living mixture of enduring French traditions and impressive innovations from across the Alps which can be found in all the French houses built before 1535 or 1540. The master masons of that period neither copied nor servilely reproduced models from across the Alps. They combined, adapted, transposed; they took their ideas where they found them.

In the same way, France did not lose its longstanding taste for the masters of the North. Think of the importance of the portrait in the history of French art of the sixteenth century. Think of the masses of what are traditionally labeled "Clouets" hanging in our museums and homes. Jean Clouet, who appears for the first time in the royal accounts in 1516, was a Fleming. And his competitor, Corneille de Lyon, also called Corneille de la Haye [of the Hague], was also a Fleming. The whole art of the French portrait in the sixteenth century, so typical, so evocative, is a Flemish art, executed by Flemings in the Flemish manner. It is interesting to note that when a few timid Italian influences appear in the French portraits in the reigns of Charles IX and Henri III, they were not introduced by Italians but by Italianate Flemings. Dimier, in his *French Painting in the Sixteenth Century,* notes this, although, quite properly, without any sign of surprise.[31]

In other words, no matter how strong the infatuation with Italy might be, such a sentiment alone could not have produced the radical change we find in French art at the start of the Renaissance. The infatuation, and what has been called the invasion of Italian art, could not have taken place before the reintroduction of an interest in classical literature had begun to change men's minds, rendering them capable of understanding, responding to, and desiring Italian art, or rather, an Italian flavor in the art of the reigns of Louis XI and Charles VIII. It is also worthy of note that this motion toward things Italian in art might have ceased had not one of the effects of the intellectual reawakening been directed toward the religious conceptions of the sixteenth century. The Reformation and the Counter Reformation were also powerful currents destined between 1540 and 1560 to overturn the old artistic and iconographic traditions of sixteenth-century French art. These things, not the Italian wars or the introduction of Italian artists into France, these things, along with the new interest in classical litera- ture, were the real causes of one of the greatest changes ever to take place in the realm of the arts in France.

Thus, a word keeps coming up by way of a conclusion to these rapid sketches: agreement, convergence, si- multaneity, and interconnections of the great currents which cross and carry along a century which at first glance seems so tumultuous, so violent, so dis- parate—a synthesis, if you like. But I prefer a simpler word: life. Life is the entire object of history. Human life too is nothing but convergence, accord, linking, synthesis; movement too, and constant interchange between forces meeting head on, the intensity of the collision sometimes giving rise to strange flames. To feel it, to understand it fully, one cannot remain at home, still and pensive without a far horizon or far- reaching thoughts, like a Flemish weaver settled in next to his warm stove for the winter. What is wanted is the open road of the wide world, where one can stop at certain controlling intersections to grasp the contra- dictory winds. In order to gain a better understanding of French art, we must know how to make the slow and deliberate journey from scrupulously detailed and concentrated Flanders to dramatic, learned, and pic- turesque Italy.

4

The Quest for God

In the old days youngsters were brought up on fine stories which were designed to be unforgettable. History was presented to us as a series of pleasant anecdotes still prepared today to answer "present" to the roll call of memory, so firmly were they stuck in our heads. No sooner do we hear "the Reformation" than the story of Brother Martin Luther comes to life before our eyes, the good monk who was sent to Rome by his convent and who saw such atrocities and abominations there that he returned brokenhearted, and from that moment, resolved to cut his ties with the Church.

We have become more exacting than we were. In schoolrooms today I suppose children of twelve are scribbling in their notebooks that although Martin Luther went to Rome he was an exemplary pilgrim, going from church to church to collect as many indulgences as possible, all the while remaining the perfect monk, revering and even admiring the pope and the cardinals whose knowledge and merits he was still praising months after his return to Germany.[1]

The anecdotal account illustrated for everyone the abstract thesis that the Reformation was the fruit of the abuses of the Church. Now, if we open the schoolbooks, proudly updated for the new century, which inform the modern enlightened public about the great religious revolution of the sixteenth century, we find the same fable. The Reformation? these books ask. It was the direct result of the decadence of the Church. The clergy at the end of the fifteenth and the start of the sixteenth century had fallen into a wretched state. Its religious education was nonexistent, its piety automatic and external, its morals deficient. From a violent attempt to remedy this lamentable situation the Reformation was born in glory.

No! a thousand times no! I do not have the time to demonstrate in detail how false this proposition is, how absurd. I do not have the time to take up, one by one, the psychological biographies of the Reformation's major figures, to show how foreign to their systems of thought the notion of "abuse" was. But at least I can ask a question: how could abuses in and of themselves give rise to anything other than more abuses? By creating a reaction? But not necessarily. There have been abuses which existed for hundreds and hundreds of years without creating any reaction of any sort whatever, so long as they were not felt to be abuses. An abuse itself does not provoke a reaction; that only happens when it is perceived as an abuse, when it becomes intolerable to those who perceive it. The change is psychological. And behind the psychological lies the social. Once again I must repeat what I have said so often before in the course of these essays: we shall find what we seek in the social order; let us look at the society of the time and we shall understand.

An entire social class was rising, prospering, growing, winning; all those bourgeois pulling themselves to the very pinnacles of the state. Look at them, listen to them, they are in charge. The Reformation was not created in full armor, it did not spring to life, blazing and passionate, from the heart of a single man however deep and broad that heart might be. The voice of Luther, two hundred years earlier, would have risen to the heavens like a stream of water from a fountain: taut and powerful at the base, but losing its strength bit by bit, slowing down until, suddenly breaking, it is lost as a fine rain. The voice of Luther, in 1517, in 1520, filled the world because, like a great echo, the voices of thousands and thousands of others, who were only waiting for a signal, were joined to his, carried his with theirs and on theirs, made it so loud, so violent, so powerful, that like the biblical trumpet, it too broke down the walls of Jericho.

Michelet said it so well that I cannot hope to do better: "Luther's impact, the force of his personality, the success of his resistance, spread through all Europe and gave impetus to the Reformation which appeared spontaneously everywhere."[2] Spontaneously, yes, but let us add that it was the child of its time, the offspring of a given society. Basically it was, in a bourgeois period, a bourgeois expression, the bourgeois expression, of religious feelings.

I

Let us look at the world of 1470 or even 1490, the eve of a new century, and examine what we see. What was the religion of a country like France, of people like the Frenchmen of that time? But first of all, can we call it *the* religion? Not really. Viewed from a distance, no doubt, there seems to have been only one religion in the France of the period, the Christian religion. But if we move closer and look into the very hearts of men?

For the great majority of the Frenchmen of the period, religion was a complex system of customs and usages, observances and ceremonies by which their entire lives were strictly conditioned. I have not mentioned "teachings" because in fact there was no one who could have or would have taught religion to the simple faithful. We must banish the France of today from our minds. In our France the priest teaches religion to the children from the time they are very young; the priest systematically and methodically teaches them their catechism. It was not so then.

Aside from a semiaristocracy who held benefices, the secular clergy consisted of a wretched proletariat of men on the spot, poor peasants not much changed by their training, a few blows from the local clergyman administered while they more or less learned to say mass and to read or recite the necessary prayers.[3] What would such a man, who knew nothing himself, have taught others? There were no seminaries then.

Only the monks considered teaching a part of their functions. They performed quite well as teachers in the cities where carefully chosen preachers, well paid, used the opportunity of Lent or Advent to indoctrinate the people in a leisurely series of sermon-lectures.[4] But in the country and in the villages a monk might pass through from time to time, and, at the request of the curate, he might give a sermon before continuing on his way. Such teaching was too loose, sporadic, and poor to have any effect. Everything was forgotten between one visit and the next. All that remained was a skeleton of rites and customs.

Religion meant going to mass, if possible every day, scrupulously casting a glance when entering and leaving at the big Saint Christopher who stood at the door of the church and protected the faithful against sudden death. Religion was to stand in the church and say the rosary while the priest officiated at the altar. It was to observe a strict fast during Lent and Ember days, to observe meatless days, to refrain from work on Sundays and holy days, to say one's prayers every day, to make two or three pilgrimages near or far in a lifetime, the best of which was to brave the winds and the tides and reach the holy land and see all the sacred places in spite of pirates, Turks, and tempests. For the pilgrim who had returned, the pilgrimage could be repeated in miniature with the aid of the stations of the cross, the devotion to which was just then developing. That was what religion meant to most people.

I hesitate to say that is all it was. Religious observances had so large a place in men's lives that all the actions of that life, even those which seem most secular to us today, like writing a will or defending a doctoral dissertation, were accomplished, so to speak, under the sign of the cross. All men's actions from birth to death were permanently controlled by religion; it regulated the smallest details of one's work, one's leisure, what one ate and how one lived; as surely as the church bells rang to signal prayers and offices, religion regulated the rhythms of human life. The Church was the center to which men rallied in times of danger and in times of joy. Every Sunday and every feast day saw the whole community assembled together, in hierarchical order. The men of the cloth were in the choir. In the seigneurial pew way up front, were the gentry, milord with his dogs, his wife, and his children. The magistrates stiffened with peasant dignity sat just behind them, then the laborers, and finally the humble folk, the valets, servants, children, and animals which were just as much at ease in the church as anywhere else. When a church or a religion has such strong and multiple holds on society, it cannot be disdainfully dismissed as mere ritual. Life itself was but a mesh of rituals.

We can go further by examining a little book, the journal of a very ordinary man who lived in the Franche-Comté, a document like a thousand others which have come down to us.[5] The name of the man in this case was Jacques Cordelier. He lived in Clairvaux, in the Jura region. As he did not belong to the clergy, he married, had children, and was subject only to normal, usual contact with the Church. He made his living selling leather. Nothing about him suggests that he belonged to an elite. In the journal we find a list entitled: "The Daily Prayers Said by Jacques Cordelier de Clairvaux, Notary, before Getting out of Bed." First he made the sign of the cross, saying: "In nomine Patris, et Filii, et Spiritus Sancti, amen"—after which he said "Veni, Sancte Spiritus, reple tuorum corda fidelium et tui amoris in eis ignem accende," with the verse "qui per diversitatem, etc." Then he said the Pater Noster; Ave Maria; Credo in unum Deum; Benedicite; Agimus tibi gratias; Confiteor, Misereatur; Ave, Salus mundi; Corpus Domini Nostri; In manus Tuas, Domine commendo; Salve Regina; from the Gospel according to John, "in principio erat"; from Luke, "Missus est angelus"; from Matthew, "cum natus est"; from Mark, "recumbentibus"; from the psalms of David, "Miserere mei, Deus, secundum"; De Profundis at full length and Oremus Fidelium; Stabat Mater; O Crux ave.

Getting out of bed, he made the sign of the cross and said: "In nomine Patris et Filii et Spiritus Sancti, amen. In nomine Domini nostri Jesus Christi crucifixi, surgo. Ille me benedicat, regat, protegat, custodiat et ad vitam perducat aeternam, amen. Abrenuntio tibi,

Satane, et conjungo tibi, Deus. Et Verbum caro factum est, et habitabit in nobis."

Then, after that: "Dignare, Domine, die isto sine peccato nos." And sometimes (but not every day) Pange, lingua, gloriosi; the hymn Magister cum discipulis; Ave maris stella; the preface of the Holy Trinity; the lamentation of Jeremiah beginning: "Recordare, Domine, quid accederit nobis."

Here we have a document which takes us far from today's habits and tells us much about the real meaning the word religion might have had in the sixteenth century.

II

The average person exists between the extremes of high and low station, of poverty and wealth. Beneath him is the mass of poor devils, miserable wretches, backward, untutored, those who work and suffer, those barely distinguishable from beasts, who, in fact, often lived more congenially among animals than in human society. Beneath the average man were vileins, scorned, ridiculed, and taunted for their clumsy awkward ways. They too were part of the Church.

Everyone went to church and everyone had a right to feel at home there. They may have felt this all the more as, once over the threshold of the House of God, the old spirit of Christian egalitarianism took over, the old spirit of the peasants' eternal marching song: "When Adam delved and Eve span, who then was the gentleman?" We are men like them, and in the eyes of God, if not in the eyes of the world, all men are equal. . . .

There they were, poor fellows, their clothing faded by years of scrubbing and wear. There they were, still worn from the hard work of the day before. While mass was said and the smell of incense rose toward God, while the nave was filled with song broken by sudden deep silences during which only the murmur of Latin from the priest's lips was to be heard, what vague dreams slowly formed behind the coarse features of their heavy heads? There were certainly no clear thoughts. What would they have thought about? Who would have filled the void of their reflections? Mass was said in Latin. Prayers, for them, were only formulae, incomprehensible incantations. No one ever really taught them their religion. They were there because that was the custom; they felt they ought to be there. They made the sign of the cross because that is what one ought to do, everyone did it, and as far back as they could remember, they had seen everyone do it. And they kneeled, rose, vaguely listened to the songs and the prayers, distracted, mouth agape, eyes glazed, all of that which approached thought fixed elsewhere.

Where? Michelet tells us:[6] in the fields, in the woods, on the moors, the fairies' oak, the cold spring where at the full moon the magic serpents and dragons came to drink at night. In the depths of their hearts they clung tenaciously to obscure and independent traditions, long believed extinguished, the surviving traditions of a latent paganism. We should not forget the broad current of popular naturalism, of instinctive pantheism, which runs through the Middle Ages and the Renaissance. For those who were susceptible to such naturalism, who succumbed to its attractions without asking where they led, Christianity had only one reply, the devil, anti-God of poor wretches. Quite suddenly heterodox groups rushed onto the scene, to be pursued, tracked down, tortured, and finally eliminated by public authority. A period of calm would follow, only to be succeeded by another similar uprising a little later, in a spot a little further on.

Often a basic communism surfaced from these troubled waters, the communism of peasants demanding water and wood as common property, the fish of the streams, the beasts of the fields, the wood of the forest, its bees and acorns, its boars and deer. Imagine a secret meeting of heavy-limbed peasants, lumbering couples in clumsy dances as they are shown in the engravings of the German old masters who lived during the social unrest of the early years of the sixteenth century. The unfocused torpor of these rudimentary beings suggests an indefinable sense of the shadowy, the unclear, the mysterious which is somewhat frightening. A great band, unaware that it was on the edge of mutiny, lived on the fringes of a civilization nearly unaware of their existence, which excluded them. But sometimes the band rose in fury, in sudden revolt against the world which crushed and rejected it. That was the extreme which lay beneath the average man.

Above him, there was the learned world, or what passed for learned. The small, closed world of the schools, of readers, those who knew how to read and had access to reading matter: manuscripts in convents, books on their shelves. In the learned world men discussed and disputed; they nourished their faith with dogmatic and theological arguments. On the eve of the Reformation we know that such people had nearly all been attracted by Ockhamism, the creation of a vigorous and hardy mind reacting to the intellectualism of a Saint Thomas Aquinas, challenging the validity of Aquinas' attempt to provide a rational interpretation for faith.[7] Ockhamism vigorously attacked all the Thomist attempts to reconcile faith and reason. It reduced Christian life to the observance of ritual and the performance of good works, while at the same time the entirety of Christianity was reduced to a series of beliefs to be accepted without question and without love; the spirit was enslaved by the letter, the layman by the clergy.

No doubt, Ockhamism in itself was neither mediocre nor minor. It could have, it might have, in another time, borne rich fruit. It amounted to forbidding, declaring inaccessible, all speculation on transcendent matters, all metaphysics. Where revelation alone was proper, human reason recognized its impotence. Faith became subject to the authority of revelation, as uncertain and indisputable from then on as dogma. But Ockhamism offered no obstacle to the study of positive, empirical phenomena. As early as the end of the fourteenth or start of the fifteenth centuries, therefore, it might have encouraged the division between faith and reason in men's minds. It is precisely this division which distinguishes modern habits of mind. Reason is accorded the regulation of this present, earthly life, the rule of law, the conduct of war and peace, of work and wealth. Religion is granted the cult of immortal hopes, the splendor of revealed truth, the promises of a future life.

Ockhamism might have done all this, in theory, but in practice the time was not yet ripe. The idea of experimental science was totally foreign to the people of the fourteenth century who had neither method nor instruments for such work. Exiled from the realm of metaphysics by Ockham, they were incapable of structuring their earthly realm. They did not so much as observe the most readily available psychological reality. They turned away from subjective observation and absorbed themselves in the most sterile and abstract study possible, formal logic and syllogistic reasoning. They built up a science of words, vain and empty, devoid of sense, which provided a butt or a straw man for all the Humanists, all the innovators, of the early sixteenth century.

It was especially serious that a thoughtless minor clergy reduced religion to a set of empty rites while a learned clergy of doctors and theologians, for very noble reasons, no doubt, but with the intransigence of logicians, withdrew into the literal and humbled observance of the commandments of the Church. The results were to be very serious indeed, for at the same time the great mass of the faithful went on living and seeking a God and a faith suited to its needs, a new spirit was at work among them.

III

Throughout the West the clergy, under the influence of the nominalism and the apologetics of Ockham, offered the faithful a stern program. They were not to understand; they were not to try to understand; they must forbid the heart and the brain the sacrilegious audacity of wanting to live or understand dogma. They must agree that dogma is unintelligible to man; following Ockham, that which man can know on this earth is not God. These authoritarian affirmations must be believed without question and without love. The formal practices ordered or sanctioned by the Church must be performed as ritual, without charity. What were the faithful to do with such a program?

For the most part the faithful we are speaking of were middle-class people with clear heads, logical and precise, capable of bold initiative; people with some schooling who knew the value of education and the liberating power of human knowledge; self-confident people, firmly grounded by their land, their houses, their gold-and-silver-filled coffers. As a consequence, they burned with desire to see a new authority, their authority, replace the old, so that they might proclaim themselves before the world for what they were: the beneficiaries and the masters of the age. The religion which was offered to them was ecclesiastical and formalistic, emphasizing authority, obedience, and incomprehension. They could not have accepted such a religion without initial malaise, and mutiny after. You will object that I have no proof of this; there are no texts which attest to this violent lack of accord between the religious feelings of a whole age, of an entire class, and the reigning theological doctrines of that age.

The answer is to be found not in texts but in works of art and in the convents. The convents were full. The eve of the Reformation is always treated as a period when Christianity was running out of breath, religious institutions were in decline, the power of the monasteries had been broken and they ceased being attractive to the world outside their walls.[8] Yet at the same time in fact the monastery cells were filled to bursting with ardent Christians, an elite who retired, worn out and disabused, from a world of churches without doctrine, schools without feeling, seeking food for their spirits and comfort for their hearts in the silent peace of the cloister. Mysticism and asceticism were the inevitable reactions against the insufficiency· of the hard and sterile doctrines of Ockhamism degenerated into terminism. No doubt they were discouraged; they gave up and this too motivated their mysticism. They felt that the evil was too widespread, the world too perverse to allow the just to live and struggle in it. This was so, but there seem to have been other

81

elements as well in the great current of mysticism which carried along so many of the elite even after the start of the Reformation.[9] Let me mention only one: Marguerite de Navarre, the sister of King François I.[10] She may be taken as exemplary of the indignation felt by those who could not be content with the nominalist attitude toward religion, the mute acceptance of the priest's words, the mechanical practice of rites and works. And that already goes far toward indicating the spirit of the times.

There is another mirror, still more expressive because it belonged not to a small group but to everyone: art, the religious art of the fifteenth century, picturesque, pathetic, and human, so well described in Emile Mâle's *Gothic Image*. What this art demonstrates is how far behind the times the theology of the day really was. How much freer, more humane, more modern the world was than we would believe from reading the philosophical and scholastic treatises of the period. Lefebvre d'Etaples, his stiff and bristling Latin still scattered with barbarisms, Lefebvre the harsh and difficult, was an almost exact contemporary of Leonardo da Vinci, or, another comparison which is never made, the exact contemporary of the great French sculptor Michel Colombe. . . . The rapidity with which the Reformation spread among the masses sometimes seems astonishing. But remember that by the time the learned, the wise preachers, and the first propagators of the Reformation decided to call for a religion closer to their needs, more personal, closer to the heart, the good people of France had already, for years and years, known an art that dwelt on the humanity of the Virgin, the anguish of the pietà, the tragedy of the *ecce homo* and entombment, through which they became accustomed to a religion stripped of priestly trappings, filled with compassion, making a direct and continual appeal to the heart.[11] And later, when these images were smashed by Protestants, they were not merely guilty of vandalism. Perhaps, in addition, in a certain sense, they were ingrates with respect to an art which had covertly prepared the way for them.

When I speak of the people, naturally I mean the middle class. Standing in the beautiful cathedral of Bourges, whose high thirteenth-century nave is unbroken by a transept, one is surrounded by little side-chapels, some dating from the thirteenth century, others from the fifteenth, so comfortable, so cheerful, so approachable. They call to mind the little rooms in which the painters of the time might have depicted the young Virgin, in an elegant posture, sweetly receiving the angel of the Annunciation. These chapels bear the names of old bourgeois families, Fradet, Beaucaire, Trousseau, Jacques Coeur, Copin, Leroy, Tullier, Aligret, who ordered the decoration, the stained glass, the altarpieces.[12] They all stand as authentic and irrefutable witnesses to the manner, human, sentimental, and pathetic, in which the enlightened bourgeoisie, rich merchants, cultured lawyers, conceived their religion and lived their faith at the very moment when Ockhamism and terminist nominalism appeared to reign triumphant.

IV

Some fled the world and took refuge within the bare walls of a monastic cell. When evening came and the day's work was done, they could lose themselves in a doctrine of renunciation and mortification, or, in a dark chapel, meditate on the painful passion of Christ beneath his crown of thorns, bathed in a sweat of blood and agony: a paltry diversion for a virile, a passionate soul. The world reborn by peace was filled with the clamor of joy and hope. The time for quiet retreat into closed cells was past. The time was come to roll up one's sleeves like Frère Jean[13] and to set to work for all one was worth.

By the end of the first quarter of the century the middle class understood the extent of its own power and energy. Using its gold and its credit, through the agency of the Fuggers, it had made an emperor, Charles V, and a pope, Leo X.[14] The printing press had begun to serve its tastes, its instincts, and its professional interests. By the end of the first quarter of the century, the middle class rose up and set to work. The clergy hardly mattered in the face of such enthusiasm. Let them step aside and make room for the bourgeois, with pride in his own reason, in his learning, in himself, his feet on the ground, his conscience clear.

"I pray to God for you, my brother," murmurs the monk to the man living in the world. "While you work with your hands and your head, while you toil to feed those who depend on you, I in my convent, humble before God, expiate for you, a sinner . . ."—a completely medieval idea which modern man proudly rejects. Who asked anything of the monk—a man, a poor fellow, weak and wretched? Let him save himself, that's quite enough. Salvation is an individual matter. Everyone will settle his accounts with God face to face at the end of his life—like the good merchant settling his accounts at the end of the month when they come due, honoring his signature without further proofs. Every time I think about such a state of mind, a little scene springs to life before me, a vivid illustration, a naive and telling story, preserved for us by anonymous witnesses.

The protagonist of the scene is Guillaume Farel, a thin little man, sinewy, raised in the Alps near Gap, endowed with enormous physical stamina. His life story reads like an adventure novel: tossed from Gap to Meaux and from Meaux to Gap, to Basle, to Strasbourg, to Metz which he fled one day disguised as a leper in a cart filled with real lepers; then on to Montbéliard, to Neuchâtel, to Lausanne and Geneva, wherever there was fighting, wherever Church and reformers clashed. . . . This short redheaded man with piercing eyes, high forehead, sharp nose, thin mouth, and a long red goatee curved like a halbard blade was the best, the surest of documents on French Protestantism before Calvin.

He was never anything but a layman. He was never ordained, never made a priest. Unlike Luther or Zwingli, he did not move from Catholic priesthood to preaching the Reform. Rather, he changed from layman to minister, and with what vigor, with what passion. But not without giving rise to astonishment, occasionally to shock even from his supporters.

The scene is in Dombresson, deep in the lovely Val de Ruz which leads to Neuchâtel along the narrow gorges of the Seyon, but which spreads out into a shell of peaceful verdure below Valangin and its old château. It was in Dombresson on a Sunday, the nineteenth of February, 1531, a winter Sunday, cold, no doubt, and snowy. But nothing would stop Farel on his rounds to spread the faith. The priest, Guillaume Gallon, was calmly saying mass. Then, strangers burst into the church, coming from Bienne, from Neuchâtel. Among them was Farel who listened for a moment and then stood, calling to the priest: "Poor fellow, won't you stop using the name of Jesus Christ blasphemously?" The priest stopped, not knowing what to

say. "Blasphemously? Really, I didn't know I was
doing that, and when I do know, I will stop." Farel
steps forward: "Give me your book and I will show
you how you entirely renounce the death and the passion of our Lord Jesus Christ, who sacrificed Himself
for us once, and need no longer sacrifice Himself more
often." Farel took the book from the priest, and with
the text in hand, showed him how he was "blasphem-
ing," until at length the priest admitted he was con-
founded and publicly confessed before all his parish-
ioners assembled that Farel was telling the truth. The
author of the account which I am following faithfully
continues: "At that moment the priest took off the gar-
ments of his office, confessing that he had made poor
use of them, repenting, and asking pity from the Good
Lord, promising God never again to say mass. And by
the strength and will of God, there and then the idols
of Dombresson were knocked down and burned."[15]

A truly symbolic scene. Guillaume Farel, at Dombresson as elsewhere, represented no one but himself.
He was only a man, an individual, however ardent,
resolute, and energetic. Behind him stood an entire social class which also performed a symbolic action.
With strong and logical hands they took from the altar,
snatched up from the hands of the speechless priest,
the book which he could repeat but could not interpret.

V

Two groups have been left out. On the one hand, in
their stronghold, the Sorbonne, the gates firmly
sealed, well protected, were Janotus de Bragmardo,
Thubal Holofernes, and their companions, the shabby,
ridiculous, and ferocious band of Sorbonnistes.[16] Pit-

iable ill-bred pedants, imprisoned by their literal-minded learning. They were at ease with it; they went no further. Grotesque perhaps, but certainly to be feared, for they were the embodiment of the Counter Reformation and, gnashing their teeth, they cast glances toward the hangman.

Representing the opposite extreme was the silent mass of peasants. What did they think? For a short time the world knew, during a brief, tragic upheaval. When Luther rose up in Germany and gave his great call for liberty, a whisper ran through the peasant masses. The pariahs, the serfs, the wretches, oppressed by all, mocked by all, made a sudden effort and rose to their feet. Their old communism rose up and they were filled with fury. The result was a series of useless revolts which shook all Germany and frightened all the world.

Those were the limits of the Reformation, the first Reformation, the middle-class and spontaneous Reformation which took place between 1520 and 1530. From above, there was the passionate resistance of the theologians; from below, the chasm of social unrest. This caused a sudden stop, great uncertainty as to what course of action should be followed in the future.

But we all know what happened next. The peasant—the nuisance whose great white teeth shining in his sunburnt face inspired fear—quickly got what was coming to him. The nobles mounted on their chargers in full armor and massacred as many as they pleased. And Luther approved. The loutish crowd grew still again. Silently they came, in body, to hear the Sunday service. But a thousand, ten thousand, a hundred thousand pyres lit throughout Europe between 1530 and 1600 tell us where they were in spirit. Each pyre represented a sorcerer or a witch whom a panicky or malicious judge caused to expiate imaginary crimes and insufficiently hidden heterodoxies.

There was a momentary triumph for the doctors of the Church who jeered, greeting the Reformation with malice as the breeding ground of a social revolution, asking with heavy irony by what right the new ministers claimed that title and from whom they received their powers. They triumphed not only because in response to the Reformation they organized a renewed Catholicism ready to go on the offensive, but also because by their opposition they forced the Reformation to become a church, to announce its limits, define its borders. This tactic was applied to some extent to Luther, most especially to Calvin. Calvin, the more clearly to mark the line which could not be crossed with impunity, marked it with tortures, with the pyre of Servetus, and the executioners' block on which Berthelier left his head.[17]

The movement appeared to come to a sudden bloody end. This was only appearance. The fact that the reformers burned Michael Servetus in no way changed the fact that tolerance was the necessary daughter of the Reformation. The Reformers might well retrench behind the narrow dogma of a strict orthodoxy. Free criticism was nonetheless the obligatory daughter of the Reformation.[18] All this was very well said quite a long time ago, in 1852, by Proudhon, in a fine passage of his *Social Revolution Demonstrated by the Coup d'Etat of December Second.*

When Luther denied the authority of the Roman Church, and with it, the Catholic constitution, and presented as a matter of faith the principle that

every Christian has the right to read the Bible and
to interpret it according to his own God-given lights,
when he has thus secularized theology, what conclusion could be drawn from this astounding claim?
The Roman Church, until then the mistress and
teacher of Christians, having erred in her doctrine,
made it necessary to assemble a council of the
true faithful who would seek the tradition of the
evangelists and would reestablish the purity and
integrity of dogma, the first need of the reformed
church, and would institute a new pulpit from
which to teach it. That was the opinion of Luther
himself, and of Melanchthon, of Calvin, of Beza, and
of all men of faith and learning who had embraced
the Reformation.[19] What followed has made it clear
that they labored under an illusion.[20] The sover-
eignty of the people, under the heading of "free
examination" which had been introduced into faith
as into philosophy, could no more permit a religious
sect than it could a philosophical system. All attempts to make unanimous declarations of the most
solemn sort which would embody Protestant ideas
were in vain. Criticism could not be bound in the
name of criticism. The negation was to continue
indefinitely, and anything that might be done to
stop it was doomed in advance, as a derogation of
principle, a usurpation of the rights of posterity, a
retrograde action. Moreover, the more time passed,
the more the opinions of theologians were divided,
the more churches were founded. And this precisely
was the strength and the truth of the Reformation.
That was its legitimate role, its future power. The
Reformation was the germ of dissolution which was
to enable people to pass imperceptibly from the
moral rule of fear to the moral rule of liberty. Bos-
suet, who thought the variety of Protestant
churches a sign of their failure—and the Protestant

ministers who blushed on account of it—all proved thereby how little they understood the spirit and the importance of this great revolution.[21]

I wanted very much to quote the whole of this passage, a fine part of a whole finer still: the great exposition, powerfully controlled, which fills the early pages of the *Social Revolution*. It can be expressed no better today, so many years later. The critical spirit is robbed of its due. The men for whom and by whom the Reformation came about might well pause at the end of the first day, stretch out in a corner of their old house, bring a few memories, a few bits of furniture from the old days, and thus make a new house as narrow and closed as the old. But it was only a pause, a provisional stop. Not all of them felt the need to observe it. They had too much energy, too much vigor, too much revolutionary virtue. They felt compelled to complete the task they had undertaken. It took three more centuries at least. But what lies at the start of this great joint development of philosophical thought, of political thought, of religious thought? A great century of which we can express once again, with greater conviction now, the fine fraternal cry of Michelet: the sixteenth century is heroic.

5

The Renaissance Merchant

The modern merchant lives a sedentary life. The shopkeeper sits behind the counter; he waits on customers and from time to time receives the visits of traveling salesmen sent by the producers. The businessman whose contacts are international and who engages in trade the world over does not travel either. Only his orders cross the globe. After all, he conducts his business in an abstract world, the world of finance, of speculation (a word whose primary meaning—abstract studies—we rarely consider). Large or small, the merchant of the sixteenth century, of the Renaissance and the Reformation, was totally different.

I

In those days there was no regular postal service. Mail was starting to be delivered by riders who changed to fresh horses at set stages on a route, but this service was only for the sovereigns and their dispatches. Private citizens generally had their letters carried by men on foot, rarely by horsemen, often by the messengers employed by a city to deal with its relations with the rest of the world. In many places the lords had the right to demand that for a very slight payment their subjects carry their letters on foot.

Even after regular postal service had been established, it worked so badly at first that this practice continued. Furthermore, there were only a few major postal routes.[1] All those who were not lucky enough to live on one had to arrange to get their mail, sometimes quite a distance, to the nearest stage of a postal route. This meant considerable wasted time and long waits.[2] To go from Lyon to Brussels toward the end of the sixteenth century, a horseman traveling at a good pace, although not at breakneck speed, needed about twenty days using a route through the Franche-Comté, Lorraine, and Luxemburg. In an emergency a merchant in Antwerp who went to the prodigious expense of sending a horseman to his Lyon office would not have received an answer in less than forty days.[3] As to the post road for such a trip between the Low Countries and Lyon, it did not even exist until 1577 when it was created by order of Don John of Austria; it went via Luxemburg, Gray, Dole, and Lons-le-Saunier.[4] From then on, the merchant seeking major new markets could delegate power to agents responsible for their own decisions and for all practical purposes independent. Alternatively, the merchant himself could travel; he could take to the road.

What difficulties that involved! Generally the unpaved, dirt roads were in a deplorable state. On rare occasions one could use a Roman road, paved for all time with indestructable masonry still to be seen today: the levées of Caesar, the *chaussées* of Brunehaut, the *chemins des Dames*.[5] But over clay or marshy terrain the trails became quagmires at the first drizzle; horses foundered to the chest, carts were soon embedded in mud to the axle. They had to be moved through the fields, thus constantly increasing the trampled area, the mudholes. Then, there were very few regular bridges: many barges, ferries, sometimes only fords, but few real wooden or stone bridges where you could cross—for a toll and a crossing fee—if the flood waters had not swept them away.[6] In short, nothing could be counted on. A single horseman was an exposed figure, especially if he had a large sum of money with him, or—the usual way of doing business—he traveled with a servant and a cart or muletrain loaded with merchandise. When Don John established the postal road from Brussels to Lyon which played so large a part in European commerce, the postmaster of Dole, Jean Theveney, was charged with supervising its construction in the Franche-Comté. He traveled over the proposed route and ordered the peasants to repair the roads and bridges to be used by the couriers. The largest mudholes were filled in with branches and bundles of sticks. Finally, he had them "uncover the woods." Those three words hold a whole chapter of social history.

A traveler, especially a stranger, was by no means safe on those roads. The guide hired—usually at the inn—to show him the way in wooded or hilly country sometimes belonged to the band of robbers who were lying in ambush ahead. The landlord himself would not scruple to hold for ransom a traveler who happened through alone or without some suggestion of protection in high places. Disbanded soldiers, marauders, plunderers swept over the countryside. A merchant who could not only be robbed of all he had with him but held for ransom as well was quite a windfall.[7]

Everything the merchant did was like that, difficult, risky, dangerous. To travel alone was a major undertaking, but to travel with a large sum of money, all in hard cash! In the merchant's purse clanked gold and silver pieces, copper and nickel coins of all sorts, weights and coinages from all over. Even a modest sum under these circumstances would represent considerable weight and volume. I recently came across an account of 1585 that mentions a payment of ten francs to a courier who took 720 francs on two horses from one town in the Franche-Comté to another less than twenty miles away. The text explains that this was because of the dangers of war and the need for a second horse—"a single horse cannot easily bear a rider and 720 francs as well." The idea that a mounted man could not carry 720 francs without the danger that his horse might break down from the weight of money, saddle, and rider, seems incredible to us but. . . . Once the sum was greater than 1,500 francs one had to have a cart drawn by at least one horse, and of course, an armed escort. The same account shows us the courier demanding fifty-five francs— a high rate—as payment for having brought 2,200 francs about thirty-five miles in a cart drawn by a horse, with the help of three mounted men: a notary, a priest, and a valet, pressed into service to make up the escort.[8] And so short a trip took three days. Prudently, money moved in this way was sometimes hidden in barrels topped with merchandise. This trick did not always protect the shipment, as is illustrated by the misadventure of a merchant's assistant in 1583 traveling from Mirecourt in Lorraine. He was sent by his master to Geneva to collect 1,800 francs. Having received the sum, he put it in a barrel filled with chestnuts, thinking that such a load would not attract attention on the road. He was wrong because the barrel opened on the road and leaked its precious cargo.[9] Generally, specie was carried in little trunks, *bougettes* or *coussinettes*, which were attached behind the saddle to the rear of the couriers. But as soon as there was any number of them, they had to be sent in a caravan.[10] If the king of Spain, Philip II, sent the Low Countries 50,000 écus by way of Savoy and the Franche-Comté, it was expected that a company of soldiers, at least, would take to the road to assure the safety of so cumbersome a treasure.

Nevertheless, the merchant had to travel. All the business of the day was conducted in a few cities, a few great central squares famous for the fairs held there at fixed intervals every year. Anyone who wanted to sell or buy there had to be there. The best known of these fairs in sixteenth-century France were those of Lyon. Their outstanding role as financial fairs where distant accounts could be settled sometimes causes us to forget their importance as mercantile fairs. Everything from everywhere was offered for sale.[11] People came from all over, Germans, Flemings, Spaniards, Italians: especially from Florence, Venice, Genoa, Lucca. To prove this, we need only open Nicolas de Nicolay's *General Description of Lyon*,[12] or better still, take from the archives of a neighboring region a few accounts of sums received and spent.

In the Departmental Archives of the Doubs, for example, we find a meticulous record of the purchases made for Philiberte de Luxemburg, the mother of the last members of the Chalons family, the princes of Orange. (Her son, Philibert, died in Italy shortly after the sack of Rome over which he presided as commander of the Imperial troops.)[13] Each time the fair was held one of the princess's servants was sent to Lyon leading a caravan. Mounted on a horse, the trusted servant preceded a mule-convoy, each animal led by a man. They went by short stages from Lons-le-Saunier to Lyon. Sometimes it took them a whole day to travel a single league through Bresse, along muddy roads which resembled lakes in spots. Nothing is so precise as the list of purchases to be made at the fair: spices, sugared almonds, sugar, a small barrel of sweet wine, a sack of almonds, a sack of rice, a sack of Marseille figs, dried currants, lots of salted fish for Lent—tuna, porpoise, cod, anchovy—saffron, three reams of good paper, sixty pounds of Paris linen, silk in skeins, fine Scottish thread, lace, ribbons, taffeta from Genoa, cloth from Holland, tablecloths, wool, scissors, needles, pins, mirrors, five hides of morocco from Spain, a hide of red leather, collars for milord's hounds, gloves for falconry, tennis balls, and on and on. And all this was to be bought from foreign merchants: grocers from Orange or Avignon for the produce of the south, Flemings for the fish, Germans or Spaniards for the rest. Nothing could better convey the difficulties and complexities then posed by a shopping expedition which today could be handled so simply, so practically. Texts like the princess's shopping list can be found by the thousands. The usual conditions under which business was conducted provided neither security nor simplicity nor reasonable speed.

There were two natural and usual consequences of this, one a moral consideration, the other economic. On the one hand the Renaissance merchant did not and could not have the placid temperament or the sedentary tastes or the narrow traditionalist views of the small shopkeeper whose horizon lies at his own doorstep. He was a traveler, an itinerant, someone who, like Ulysses, had seen and daily saw the habits and customs of many men, who left a few of his prejudices in each of the lands to which one after the other his adventurous life led him. He liked such a life precisely because of its risks and its variety, its chance encounters and its contrasts. Great feasts one day, poverty and peril the next. The moral and intellectual type of the merchant was soon clearly and precisely drawn in the literature of the day. We see him in the beginning of the nineteenth story of the *Cent Nouvelles Nouvelles,* in a scene where a good and rich London merchant, stout of heart, courageous, is moved by a "burning desire to see the world, to know and acquaint himself with the many events which happen daily everywhere." He sets off well provided with money and "a great abundance of merchandise." For five years he travels before returning to his wife, but soon the wandering life calls him forth again. "He dreamed of adventures in strange lands ruled by Christians or Saracens, and tarried not, so that ten years went by before his wife saw him again." It was a short stay at home since, after two such trips he "did not yet have his bellyful of travel," and soon set off once again. . . .

From the very conditions we have been describing it must be clear that a specialized trade was not yet possible. Traveling the open road, necessarily traveling, the merchant bought what he found cheap and sold what he could sell at a profit. There was no other rule and no other choice. If he had a taste for commercial risk, maritime trade would satisfy it. But even if he was prudent, even if he had no special ambition, he did not buy and sell only one sort of goods. His aim, big or small, according to his desires and his abilities, was to corner the market, an operation we know all too well today.

Monopoly and hoarding to corner the market: these are the ideas which appear again and again in sixteenth-century texts. They are the constant preoccupation, the great complaint, of buyers and consumers forced to submit to the merchant's conditions. They are the preoccupation, the great exercise of skill, the triumph of the merchant. It was not only princes of commerce, the stars, men like the Du Peyrats of Lyon who tried to monopolize the entire spice trade, or Roquette of Toulouse, who in 1502 centralized the entire drapery trade of Roussillon and Catalonia, or Conte, the fur trader who seized control of all commerce in pelts from the Levant by reaching an "understanding" with the Neapolitan importers. . . . There were also thousands of little and middle-sized traders more bold than rich who roamed the countryside and snapped up grain, wine, butter, cheese, skins, fat, or wax for candlemaking. They descended upon villages with a train of carts and loaded what could be got from the peasants by threats, fraud, or persuasion. Often they had a little army of buyers under their orders, capable of creating a scarcity of goods, preparing for increased costs, doing what they could to boost prices. Or else, the merchant operated by gaining control of the entire export production of the peasants of a given region. For example, around 1570 some Nurembergers bought up all the thread and cloth produced around Lyon to sell wholesale in the major centers. Edicts denounced such practices in vain. They forbade abusive practices and monopolies, but had no more effect in the sixteenth century than they do today. The lure of profit is too strong, and, furthermore, at a time when total production was insufficient and product movement was filled with problems, monopolies were almost a necessity. It was, in any case, inevitable, one might almost say doubly so, from the human and the material points of view.

We begin to have a clearer picture of the kind of man the merchant was. He was florid and animated. The merchant, in the last analysis, was a soldier. He was, at least in the etymological sense of the word, an adventurer. After years and years of nineteenth-century jokes and cartoons the shopkeeper and the grocer seem to us the most placidly bourgeois of all tradesmen. The sixteenth-century merchant, on the contrary, was called upon to make prompt decisions, to exhibit extraordinary physical and moral energy, boldness, and resolution. He had to be that way, otherwise he would have been crushed by the demands of his profession. From another point of view, he pursued profit in all possible ways, without too many moral scruples; to be considered an honest man he had only to observe the essential rules of his profession with respect to other merchants, especially as regards settling accounts. Finally, he was not a specialist. He was not a sedentary or passive middleman. He had to find his merchandise, create his trade. Above all, he was a speculator. Inasmuch as he was successful in his attempts to profit from hoarding, he speculated. Because his commercial activities never really seemed enough, he speculated. And, in addition to trade, he speculated in currency and money lending. Manipulator, coin changer, and usurer: those were the three simultaneous faces then of the figure who today merely buys from one source to sell to another.

II

To be properly understood, sixteenth-century financial speculations should be considered as an extension of attempts to control supply, to monopolize, common practices among the merchants of the time. Contemporary methods of producing coin also enter the picture.[14]

Today with our advanced machines we can easily

mint coins which correspond almost exactly to the legal model. They leave the presses with the prescribed diameter and rarely vary in weight or metal content. In addition a milled edge and ring molding on both sides surrounds each coin. The edge bears an inscription or other identifying mark. Any attempt at fraud which obscures one or the other of these marks would be immediately apparent to the eyes of the least suspicious observer.

At the end of the fifteenth century and at the start of the sixteenth, on the other hand, coins were still hammered. This primitive means did not generate much pressure, so a very malleable alloy had to be used. As soon as it contained a grain too much copper the coiners complained that they were unable to work the harder metal. In an order of the eleventh of September, 1521, the emperor Charles V affirmed that he had prescribed the striking of a fourteen carat gold carolus, alloyed by seven and one half carats of silver and two and one half carats of copper.[15] The coiners could not work the metal, so it was necessary to reduce the proportion of copper to two carats. Furthermore, since the hammer struck uneven blows on very soft metal, the blanks varied, so that despite the best efforts of the workmen to the contrary, there was considerable difference in size and weight among the finished coins.

These differences, it goes without saying, did not escape the practiced eyes of the merchants, goldsmiths, gold-leaf-makers, refiners, money changers, bankers, and other businessmen. They sorted the coins. The lightest were left in circulation. They withdrew the heaviest to clip them or attack them with acid. Gold obtained by these methods was melted into ingots and returned to the workshop or sold abroad.[16] The profits from such an operation could be considerable, and for this reason such practices were universal. Everywhere, in all countries, there were complaints about the activities of *billoneurs,* as they were called in France, *Kippers* or *Wippers* in Germany—all rascals who did not think twice about the empty threat of being boiled alive as a counterfeiter, or at the least, fined and harshly imprisoned. Nor did anyone consider seriously the remedies proffered by the economists or the suggestion, for example, of Bodin that henceforth money should be cast as the Greeks, Romans, Hebrews, Persians, and Egyptians had produced their coins, a much cheaper and easier method by which the coins would be more true to round.[17] Empty proposals. For centuries men had fiddled with coins, sometimes causing serious monetary crises in times when gold was rare. That is why, after each issue, a country was nearly instantly stripped bare of a portion of its good coins. That is why virtue was always punished and vice always recompensed. A state which obstinately struck good money, of good alloy, saw that money leave as soon as possible. A swarm of profiteers descended on the land, their bags and trunks crammed with debased coins of inferior alloy which they offered simple, naive country people in exchange for the good local money. Their profits were enormous.

It should be remembered that at this time every country had its own monetary policy. There is no question but that all the states of Europe had been bimetallists since the second half of the thirteenth century. At about that time, more or less everywhere, gold coins came back into use. But not all countries used the same ratio of value between gold and silver. It was fixed for a long time at 1:15.5 in the countries belonging to the Latin Union.[18] By the sixteenth century it varied from country to country and, within a country, from period to period. Money belonged to the sovereign. It was part of his patrimony, one of his personal, all but private, resources. He had the right to fix the *taille* as he wished: to decide how many coins should be struck from the weight of precious metal taken as a base unit (the mark). He had the right to set the alloy, which might be pure (in which case it was twenty-four carats for gold and twenty-four grains for silver) or more or less impure. Finally, he had the right to determine the legal value of his coinage.

Today such a procedure would be senseless. Money of account and actual coins coincide: we count by francs, but the franc actually exists and is really worth a franc. In the sixteenth century the livre was the unit of account, but there was no real livre. There was a whole series of coins, some gold, some silver, all of different shapes, weights, alloys, and faces. In issuing them the sovereign assigned them a value expressed in livres, sous, and deniers—that is, in money of account. But this value was not indicated on the coins themselves. It was fixed by edict, by decision of the prince. Another edict, another decision of the prince, might modify its value. In fact, such changes were frequent. The monetary history of sixteenth-century France is full of them. There continued to be repeated shrinking of the value of coins. That is, decisions of the sovereign caused, for example, a gold coin of twenty-three carats, worth, let us say, three livres, to contain henceforth only twenty-two carats while it continued to be worth three livres. It is immediately apparent that such practices, often repeated, frequently occurring, played into the hands of the hoarders of metal and coins, the merchants. The landed nobility lost by it because they were owed rent or other payments in sums expressed in money of account. Furthermore, the continual and arbitrary interventions of the prince had the effect of shifting the relation between the value of gold and silver. It changed from country to country, to the speculators' advantage. Gold went where its value was the highest, and silver did the same. Merchants hoarded these metals in the regions where their value was relatively low and exported them into those where it was relatively inflated. It is worth mentioning as well that during this period not gold but silver was the real sign of wealth, the basic metal. The French language still reflects this today. A rich man is said to have *argent,* silver, not gold.[19] Gold was the merchants' metal, the metal of commerce, of export, of banking, and therefore, of speculation. It owed this position to qualities inherent in it: it had more value in less volume and therefore was better suited than silver to big payments and to export. It was also easier to disguise and bring across closely watched borders. . . .

In the sixteenth century France tended to attribute more value than its neighbors did to gold with respect to silver. According to Soetbeer the average ratio of value of gold to silver in Europe from 1501 to 1520 was 1:10.75; from 1521 to 1540 it was 1:11.25. In France in 1519 it was 1:11.76, and in 1542, 1:11.82.[20] In other words, with the same quantity of gold during those years more silver coins could be bought in France than in Italy or Spain. Or, putting it another way, a given quantity of silver could be purchased with less gold in France than in Italy or Spain. The result was a continual flow of gold toward France. This flow did not take place without leaving some very considerable profits in the hands of those who directed it (that is, the merchants). And that is why in Italy, in Spain, in Portugal,

103

in England, in Germany, everywhere, there were complaints in the sixteenth century that gold was fleeing the country, drawn to France by the high exchange rates there.[21]

To this it must be added that France, a rich and productive country, was a great exporter, the country where, in times of peace, people came to get what they could not get elsewhere. Contemporaries remarked on this, Bodin among them. In his *Response to the Paradoxes of Monsieur de Malestroict on the Subject of Coinage,* he shows us the Spaniard constrained "by inevitable forces" to buy wheat, cloth, textiles, dye, paper, books, woodwork, "and other manufactured items" in France. That is why the Spaniard went to "the ends of the earth looking for gold and silver and spices" in order to be able to buy what he needed from France. In the same way, the Englishman, the Scotsman, and "all the peoples of Norway, Sweden, Denmark, and the Baltic coast where there are many mines dig deep into the earth to find the metals to buy our wines, our saffron, our prunes, our dye, and above all, our salt which is a manna, God-given with little labor."[22]

These interesting remarks cast light on many sides, on many great questions of history. Spain, then, might sometimes conquer France on the field of battle with the immense combined Imperial forces. But on the field of commerce, Spain was at France's mercy. It needed to buy all those things which it could not itself produce; it had to pay a stiff price. Spain preferred to pay the price in gold, not only because gold was more convenient for large payments, but also because, as opposed to France, Spain tried to keep the value of silver as high as possible. This metal was abundant in the Iberian peninsula. Once the Potosi mines were being

fully worked, silver became a truly Spanish metal.[23]
This explains why Charles V always showed a degree
of reluctance to raise the price of gold coins with respect to silver, even though he was aware that only
such a change could prevent the metal's exportation.

Furthermore, for Castile the movement of gold out
of the country was less serious than for Italy, since
Spain was supplied from the New World not only with
silver but with Mexican and Peruvian gold as well. Levasseur figures that until 1545—that is, until the discovery of the Potosi mines—Spain got about as much
gold as silver from her colonies.[24] It is nonetheless true
that in 1537 Charles V was forced in his turn to reduce
the gold content of Spanish coins just as Venice,
Genoa, and Florence had earlier found themselves
forced for analogous reasons to change their fine
ducats and florins into écus-sols. A Castille écu was
created of twenty-two carats, a weight equal to the
best écus of Italy and France. This measure stopped
speculation. It did not slow the exodus of Spanish gold
which continued because of a commercial exchange
that generally did not operate in Spain's favor, and because of the ruinous wars into which the Catholic
Kings drew their country.

As we have seen, when the artists of the sixteenth
century wanted to paint "the merchant" they had
ample reason for presenting him, as did Quentin
Metsys in his pleasing little painting in the Louvre,
busy weighing gold, with an expression at once serious
and absorbed, appropriate for the financier. His wife
at his side, prettily capped in black, distractedly leafs
through a marvelously illuminated Book of Hours, but
not without casting sidelong glances at the gold coins
which her husband is meticulously weighing and
reweighing. The weighing of gold is a kind of sacra-

mental act of the merchant of the Renaissance. It was not Quentin Metsys alone, or only his emulator and continuator, Marinus, in the careful paintings identified by Monsieur de Mely, who depicted that familiar scene.[25] We see it in the works of Corneille de Lyon (also the attribution of Monsieur de Mely). In Jost Aman's large engraved allegory of commerce one sees in the foreground, next to the accountants' desks and the cashiers' counter, a big money-changing table on which two clerks are carefully counting sacks filled with coins, some of which fill the pans of the balance. It is those gold-weighing scales which are the true symbol of commercial activity of the sixteenth century.

III

Once the merchant had all the gold and silver in his cash-boxes, what did he do with it? Did he limit its use merely to broadening his commercial activity, his personal business? Not in the least. Commercial activity under the conditions we have been describing could not be regular and continuous. It was necessarily intermittent. Each commercial action, each big purchase or big sale must be seen as an operation long and carefully prepared, executed decisively, boldly, perseveringly. But once it was finished, a new one must be begun, which might be entirely different, which would probably not involve the same kind of goods, and which, in any case, would be carried out under different conditions from the first. Between all these distinct operations there were periods of calm, of respite. Could money be allowed to rest undisturbed in the coffers of the merchant during these breaks in commercial activity? That would be contrary to its nature. Money must "work." So the merchant lent it. But to whom? and how?

First we must set aside a series of special procedures: I mean capital invested by a silent partner. The merchant could and often did lend to other merchants. There are many examples of this practice. Some can be found in the very interesting book in which P. Masson has studied the coral companies established in sixteenth-century Marseille to conduct coral fishing on the Algerian and Tunisian coasts.[26] The archives of the Department of the Isère have fortunately and unexpectedly preserved these accounts. But I would prefer to examine an even more typical and characteristic example. A few short, practical sixteenth-century manuals of commerce and accounting have come down to us. It is generally very instructive to leaf through them. One of the most interesting and best known is entitled, *Brief Instructions on Keeping Account Books in Double Parts*. It was the work of a Pierre de Savonne, a native of Avignon, and was printed in many editions. I refer here to the fourth, revised in several places, and with a sixth book added, which was printed in Lyon by Jean de Tournes in 1608. Pierre de Savonne proposes the following example: three firms of merchants incorporate for three years, the Couvat brothers, partners in Marseille, Gaudin in Lyon, and Renaud, also of Lyon. The example is pure fiction, but you must see that it is not unlikely or chimerical, that the author is interested in verisimilitude. When a problem is posed, it makes sense not to go beyond probability, especially in a science so precise as accounting. So, we have our three parties to the agreement. The Couvets bring 25,000 écus in cash, Gaudin brings 12,000 and Renaud 10,000, part in cash, part in goods.

The corporation is formed with a capital of 47,000 écus d'or soleil.[27] But who are the Couvet brothers? Simply money lenders, rich merchants who are silent partners in a commercial venture in which they will have neither responsibility nor direct control. In other words, they lent their money to other merchants so that they might make it work. And the results of the corporation imagined by Pierre de Savonne are interesting to examine. The starting capital was 47,000 écus d'or, of which two-thirds was in money. The corporation lasted three years. At its dissolution, the accounts were drawn up. Pierre Gaudin's balance was 21,371 écus (on an investment of 12,000, partly in goods). Renaud's share was 18,364 écus (on an investment of 10,000, partly in goods). The Couvet brothers' return on their investment of 25,000 écus is 39,456. The total profit in this presumably fictional but realistic example is 21,592 écus on 47,000 écus working for three years. All told, that is quite a respectable profit. It comes to about 15.5 percent a year. Once again, the example is hypothetical, but not far-fetched.[28]

The merchant did not limit himself to acting as a silent partner in the affairs of other merchants. He also lent in the more usual sense, to private individuals.

The merchant in the small town or city received an unending line of country people caught short of cash. What did they want? A little money to deal with their most urgent needs, the purchase of grain, of livestock, or of hay. In the merchant they generally found a source both of the things they wished to buy and the money with which to buy it. But at what price?

The merchant did not actually lend money. The Church forbade lending money for interest. The interdiction had only a theoretical value, but in that sense it was respected.[29] The difficulty was overcome most often by means of what was known as the "constitution of rent." A peasant needed 100 francs to buy livestock. He promised to give the merchant a certain quantity annually of wheat, oats, rye, wine, or cheese, in exchange for which he got the money he wanted. Obviously the merchant's calculations assured that the value to him of the goods he was to get was never smaller than the sum he loaned. Of course there was a loophole. If the wheat harvest turned out to be exceptionally abundant the year that the peasant and the merchant made their deal, wheat would be of very little value, prices would be very low. The merchant might not make very much profit. But as he had a stock, he was not forced to sell just then. In his storehouse the peasant's wheat would join that of others. The merchant would wait a year, or two if need be, until a poor harvest drove up prices and he could sell his grain at a profitable price. And then, the merchant rarely made loans except at discount. The peasant who borrowed 100 francs in reality took away with him only eighty. Finally, the merchant sold everything. What would the peasant do with the sum he borrowed? Buy livestock? The merchant would: (1) lend him the sum, at discount, and with a fully legal *constitution de rente*; (2) obligate him, as an absolute condition of the loan, to buy his livestock from the merchant who, of course, would sell it at twice its normal price. All of this is only an outline. But the outline was traced following thousands and thousands of documents. The archives of our law courts, the archives of our provincial *parlements,* are filled with texts on this subject. One has only to open a register of criminal actions brought toward the middle of the sixteenth century to find these practices described over and over

109

again in suits against usurers. So there were legal moves against this from time to time, when the voices of the poor shorn sheep, the people who had been exploited, picked clean, despoiled of all they had, rose so loud that the powers-that-be renewed their efforts to enforce laws against usury. They had about the same success as they might have today, and I leave you to decide whether they presented a serious obstacle to those who wanted to continue such practices.

The merchant did not make loans to peasants alone. Clearly the peasant could not fight back. He was easy to intimidate, to silence. He was ignorant and defenseless once out of his village. He was the ideal debtor. But the merchant might also lend to a bourgeois temporarily short of cash, or to a nobleman who had just suffered one ⸜f those unforeseen calamities which were particularly noble calamities: a ransom to pay, equipment to replace, the purchase of a war horse, major repairs to the seigneurial manor. Finally the merchant might lend to a city, and that was generally the lowest risk loan of all, the way a man with children to provide for might use his money. While all of these operations did not offer the side-profits of lending to peasants, they still earned the lender a good rate. The normal rate of such loans was never less than 8 percent at mid-century. And that was exceptionally low. Rates of 12.5 percent, 13.3 percent, and even 16.6 percent were common, normal, perfectly licit. They left room for comfortable profits and, in addition, were generally low-risk loans.

Finally, going a step further up the ladder, the merchant might lend, not to poor country folk (deals without prestige but undoubtedly the most profitable of all if one was of the temperament to follow them up close and hard), nor to generally solvent clients like bourgeois, noblemen in difficulty, or cities negotiating some short-term loan, but rather to sovereigns, to princes, to the state. Loans of this kind were both prestigious and delicate operations, bringing high risk and the promise of high profits. They began with honors and favors, influence at court, colossal gain, a princely style of life. But they sometimes ended at the Montfaucon gallows.

To understand this we must first understand how the sixteenth century conceived of government finance. Today a state gets the money it needs in the most straightforward way, either by selling treasury bonds to large financial establishments and rich men for that part of their capital they do not want to tie up for the long term, or by borrowing from the public. The loan is infinitely divisible. The state's creditors are legion. They are citizens and foreigners, big capitalists and small savers, individuals and groups. They have confidence in a loan made to a nation or its representatives. The wealth of the nation itself appears to be collateral, and in normal times the creditors of the state ask no more. In the sixteenth century, things were different.

First of all, the state, from a financial point of view, did not exist. There was the sovereign.[30] He was an individual, like any other, sometimes a good manager, sometimes a spendthrift, sometimes honest and straightforward, sometimes devious. In any case, only as an individual could he ask for credit. In 1530 it was not France that borrowed money, but François I, the prince, who inspired more or less confidence in the lenders. And when France needed money in 1530, François I, who financially speaking was France, had to find a lender in exactly the same way as the lowest gentleman of his chamber when he wanted to buy a war horse and did not have the money in his wallet. He had to find a lender. He had to conduct long negotiations about the conditions of the loan. He had to promise to repay the loan in the shortest time possible. He often had to give pledges, to assign either a general or a particular part of his revenues, or give the signature of someone who would stand surety for him. There were no official lenders. The king knocked on all doors, begged from all purses. Financial establishments by themselves big enough to answer to his needs did not yet exist. And if there had been any, they would not have helped him all the time, for that would have left them without sufficient guarantees.

What was, at any given moment, the exact financial condition of the sovereign? No one knew precisely, not even the king himself. Had he already borrowed, and from whom, how much, with what conditions? It was not known. So, the king, who would have got nothing if he had always turned to the same sources, solicited all comers. The capital of the nobles or the clergy or royal officers or merchants was equally acceptable. In sixteenth-century Europe, there were two or three big commercial centers where business of this kind was transacted. For France it was Lyon, Lyon where François I most often negotiated his loans. For the Imperial coalition it was Antwerp, Antwerp where Charles V negotiated his loans, either directly or through the intermediary of those who represented the Low Countries. From whom did they borrow? From French or Italian or German merchants, as the case might be. And deals were not easily made; the atmosphere was not one of easy confidence.

The usual rate of interest was very high. Loans were always short-term ones, the time between two fairs, or at most, and very rarely, a year. Interest was generally

3 percent a quarter, the time between fairs, or 12 percent a year. When the appointed time came, the next fair, the sovereign most often could not pay. The loan was extended to the following fair, but naturally this extension was not without cost. Furthermore, bankers generally got a free supplementary grant of between 2 and 4 percent a year to cover their costs and risks. Usually it was not they themselves who made the loans. They acted as brokers. They furnished the king with money borrowed from other merchants or rich individuals. Such a deal was worthwhile, for example, if they managed to borrow money at 10 percent and lend it at 12, to which must be added the 2 to 4 percent of the free supplement. And there was the variable profit that might be made from currency fluctuations at the time of repayment, for they generally managed to be repaid at the going rate rather than the official one. When everything has been included, the nominal 12 percent becomes 16 percent at the very least, sometimes 18, with luck 20 percent. In six or seven years, if the sovereign had been unable to pay the initial loan, the sum was doubled.

It is not surprising that, in the end, sixteenth-century states bent under the weight of such obligations. Nor is it surprising that bankruptcy was a constant temptation to kings and emperors. The lenders knew this and made allowances for it. The best-backed loans, the most solemn engagements undertaken "on the king's word" were precarious. Some day the king might decide that in paying interest to his creditors he was committing a great sin, contravening the canonical interdiction against usury, and to put his conscience at rest, would not only refuse to pay the interest but also make the lenders return what he had already paid. Such a situation is not imaginary. In

1545 the creditors of François I demanded letters from the king stating that the "gifts," that is, the supplemental interest paid to the king's various creditors, would be considered regular obligations—and that the merchants would not have to worry about the payment of those due either in the past or the future. Furthermore, whenever the king was sick or when he was simply old, his creditors feared that he might die. If he did, what would happen to the promises he had given them? Would they be recognized by his successor? Might not the new king declare total or partial bankruptcy?[31] When François I needed money in 1546, he could borrow only on condition that the dauphin be jointly responsible for the loans: the lenders quite openly expressed their fear of being tricked.

Anyone who wants to know how plainly creditors spoke or wrote to those who were in their debt, even if the debtor's name was François I, has only to read, among many others, the interesting letter Monsieur Vial published in the *Revue d'Histoire de Lyon.* François I had borrowed 17,187 écus on April 26, 1522, from John Cleberger, the "good German" of Lyon. The sum was repayable in four installments to be drawn from the revenues of the salt tax. When the time came for the first payment, none was made. Cleberger, a respectable native of Nuremberg, had become a naturalized citizen of Bern, the better to do business in Lyon.[32] (Certain subterfuges were not invented yesterday.) Without delay, Cleberger called upon the Council of Bern to come to his defense. On July 6, 1527, the Council acceded to the demands of its adoptive son, and did in fact send François I a letter which should be read in its entirety, but from which I will give the essential passage here.

We marvel that you care so little to carry out your promises, considering that it does not profit your honor to take away what you have given by letters and seals whereby your royal majesty might receive, should this be known, great damage, not only in our country, but among all the princes and imperial cities of Germany, which we would regret.

A harsh communication, without any softening phrases. In the classic work of Ehrenberg on the century of the Fuggers, a similar letter can be found, written by Jacob Fugger, the great Augsburg banker, to the Emperor Charles V.[33]

But regardless of the risks, doing business with princes remained very tempting for merchants. There were surely profits to be made. And then, very often, it was hard to refuse. Cleberger, as a foreigner, could have recourse to the Magnificent Lords of Bern, and he did not fail to do so. But Frenchmen had no hope of such recourse. They were forced to remain enmeshed. And there they sometimes stayed; that is the often tragic story of the biggest French merchants of the period, and, to mention only one who might be taken as a type, it is the story of Semblançay.

Jacques de Beaune, known to history by the name of his estate at Semblançay, was a merchant of Tours.[34] He was the son of Jean de Beaune, who appears in 1454 as provisioner to the House of Angoulême, and who, ten years later, was one of the biggest businessmen in the kingdom. Jean de Beaune's specialty was cloth, but he dealt in other things as well. We find him, for example, taking an active part in the great commercial undertakings of Louis XI. When Louis XI had four ships built in 1464, the Saint Martin, the Saint Nicolas, the Saint Louis, and the Saint Mary, to follow the four ships that Jacques Coeur had already sent off on the Mediterranean, Jean de Beaune joined Geoffroy le Cyvrier of Montpellier, J. de Cambrai of Lyon, Nicolas Arnoul of Paris, and Jean Plat of Bruges to provide the necessary capital. It was, as can be seen, a broadly based international corporation of great merchants.

Jean de Beaune, then, was among those who were charged with receiving goods brought by ship from the Levant and putting these goods into circulation. In 1470 it was he who provided the first raw silks for the Italian silk-makers whom Louis XI had brought from the other side of the Alps to settle first in Lyon, then in Tours. Later, with his son-in-law, Jean Briçonnet, he sent to London at the request of the king 25,000 écus worth of spices, cloth of gold, and silk, in an attempt to recapture direct access to the English market, freeing the French from the need to trade through Bruges. Deals at once commercial and political were joined by a financial element. The king drew Jean de Beaune into the seizure of the goods of Cardinal Balue and Philippe de Commines.[35] In 1473 Jean lent the king 30,000 livres, half of which was provided by his son-in-law Briçonnet, to retake Perpignan from the king of Aragon.[36] He was treasurer for the household of the dauphin, Charles (the future Charles VIII). Profit, riches, honors naturally followed. When the king created the position of mayor of Tours in October 1471, Jean de Beaune was the first to hold that office. He married money. He had a house, stables, gardens in Tours, farm land, vineyards, house and property in Touraine worth nearly 23,000 livres. Jean de Beaune was the sketch, the rough draft, the preparation. His son, Jacques de Semblançay, was the finished picture.

First, Jacques was also a merchant draper, but we have just seen in Jean de Beaune how broad the implication of such a profession might be. Jean had three sons. One joined the clergy and the other two, Guillaume and Jacques, were drapers. He left six daughters: six sons-in-law were drapers or financiers. Jacques, having followed his father into the business, married Jeanne Ruzé, a caste marriage, money marrying money. The Ruzés were, along with the Beaunes, the Briçonnets, and the Berthelots, the elite of Touraine's rich bourgeois merchant class. The intricate interlacing of alliances by marriage among these families suggests the coherence of their circle, the world of big business and high finance.

Jacques began as a salesman. He sold broadcloth, silk, wool, and linen to several princes. He was the official draper to the houses of Orléans, Angoulême, and La Tremoille. In association with Briçonnet, he sold, between October 1490 and January 1492, 41,127 livres worth of cloth to Charles VIII. At the same time, like his father, he was engaged in financial deals, lending money, keeping his capital at work.

The year 1492 marked a new stage. He was appointed treasurer general to Duchess Anne of Brittany who had become queen of France in 1491. Then, in September of 1492, he added the duties of master of the duchess' household. Jacques de Beaune was no longer a bureaucrat who followed orders. He was a royal administrator who gave them. As such he was paid, deservedly, 24,000 livres for the treasury, and 2,000 livres for the household. He managed an ordinary budget of 100,000 livres granted the duchess by the king, to which were added annual supplements of 20,000, 40,000, 50,000 livres sometimes. And then, these sums were not paid in cash. They were rights to collect designated receipts—that is, Jacques de Beaune was supposed to do what he could to get the money which, in theory, he was intended to have. Moreover, Anne de Bretagne spent freely, and her squandering caused the treasurer a great deal of work. From January to September 1492, she spent 277,750 livres; from October 1492 to September 1493, 201,199 livres. These expenses were covered by a regular annual budget of 100,000 livres. She spent money for the arts, for luxuries, for her constant travel and that of her court: a great train of carts for baggage and carts for travelers, litters filled with maids and ladies of honor, an army of guides, ushers, boatmen to help cross rivers, horsemen for an escort, people to assure the lodging of the court, and on and on. The administrator of all these people and services was Jacques de Beaune. It was he who advanced money when funds had run out, he who bought back the jewels the queen had pawned in Lyon during the Naples war.[37] It was he who provided dowries for the maids of honor to whom the queen gave sums she did not have. It was he who lent his mistress 20,000 livres in 1495–96. He was an administrator, not a bureaucrat, but still a merchant and a private citizen who was not forbidden to make his own money work as he saw fit. Already he had one foot in the world of the court and politics. In his person commerce acceded to state honors and public offices.

Another barrier was breached in 1496. Jacques de Beaune became one of the four generals of finance, that is, one of the four sovereign administrators of the revenue produced by the *taille,* the *aides,* and the *ga-*

belle.[38] These four men alone could authorize the use of such moneys by their signatures. This was the source of their importance, their power, their standing. They were neither ministers nor great officers of the crown nor gentlemen. Merchants remained ordinary commoners despite their ennoblement and the estates from which they took their names. But they were much more powerful than ministers and great officers of the crown. Such men were at their service, for there was not one of them who did not need the generals of finance to assure the speedy processing of their pensions and appointments. Without them nothing could be done. Lords, cities, sovereign courts needed them to pay wages; poets and courtiers needed them to receive their grants. They were flattered, showered with gifts and offers of hospitality from all sides. Those were the honors. But there was also profit.

Semblançay, the administrator of royal finances, remained at the same time a private citizen who engaged in speculation and who made money. Most visibly he had what amounted to a private bank, at which the beneficiaries of royal generosity negotiated the letters of payment granted them by Semblançay himself. These letters were assigned to various individual tax collectors or *grenetiers*[39] in the kingdom. So as to avoid going great distances and engaging in complicated procedures, the recipients of royal letters of payment generally requested one of the generals of finance to advance them the money. In exchange for a certain percentage, they left to the general the task of getting the money from the tax collectors.[40] Semblançay also found loans for the sovereign at tight moments. He himself lent to the king, and sometimes large sums. For example, in 1503 under Louis XII wars were being waged everywhere, in Naples, Perpignan, Bayonne, Calabria, and Catalonia. Finances were at their lowest ebb. The queen lent 50,000 livres, Jacques de Beaune, 23,000, his father-in-law Guillaume Briçonnet, the duke of Nemours, and the Marechal de Gye, 20,000 each. You need not suppose that Jacques de Beaune was in danger of losing his money. He had a thousand potential means of having it back a hundred times over. He made use of them, so much, and so well that one day he became so rich . . . that the accumulated hate burst forth and the king had him thrown into prison where he was made to cough up some of his money before finally being hanged at the Montfaucon gallows for dereliction of duty. Semblançay had done nothing but play the game according to the rules.

The example of Semblançay is typical. It was characteristic of an entire large social movement. At the lowest level, the small merchant selling at a fair lent his profit at interest and made money from those poorer than he. At the top, the court merchant, become princely administrator or general of finance, implicated in the highest dealings of politics and diplomacy, moved in the same circle as kings and queens. Both are part of the same pyramid.

Because financial dealings were not at that time separate from commercial dealings, the profession of merchant held the promise of greater things. From such beginnings came enormous fortunes like those of the Ponchers, the Briçonnets, the Beaunes in Paris and Tours, the Du Peyrats in Lyon, the Pincés in Angers, the Bonalds and Vigouroux in Rodez, the Roquettes and Assezats in Toulouse. All lived like princes, lavish princes, Renaissance princes. They did not merely earn huge sums, they spent them as well. All have left their names in the history of the arts because they all filled their fine houses with collections of furniture, fabrics, jewels, works of art truly worthy of a prince. Beneath them there were many lesser merchants who had taken 80,000 or 100,000 livres of capital from their business, bringing them a yearly income of 5,000 to 10,000 livres, as much as could be expected from a county or a barony, the income of good bishopric or an abbey. In theory such men were as rich as the richest gentlemen of their provinces. In practice they were richer because they were not encumbered by the same obligations.

A new aristocracy was on the rise, an aristocracy of parvenus which the old aristocracy refused to recognize, which it envied and hated, yet which it was ready enough to marry into. The aristocracy of capital, of precious metals, was mistress of gold. In a world more and more affected by the thirst for gold, in a world where economic and financial problems were coming more and more to the fore, it was thereby, in part, mistress of Europe's destiny.

Notes

1. The Silhouette of a Civilization

1. Febvre wrote an article on the history of the word "civilization," which, surprisingly, was not used in French before 1766 (and made its first appearance in English at about the same time). "Civilisation, le mot, l'idée," *Première Semaine internationale de synthèse,* 2d fasc. (Paris, 1930), pp. 1–50; reprinted in Eng. trans., Lucien Febvre, *A New Kind of History,* ed. Peter Burke, trans. K. Folka (New York, 1973), pp. 219–257.

2. Jules Michelet, *Introduction à l'histoire universelle: Tableau de France; Préface à l'histoire de France* (Paris, 1831).

3. See Lucien Febvre, *A Geographical Introduction to History,* trans. E. G. Mountford and J. H. Paxton (London, 1932), especially part 2, chap. 3.

4. Sebastian Munster's *Cosmographei oder Beschreibung aller Länder* (Basle, 1541) was probably the first of these geographies, usually heavily illustrated with maps of countries and provinces as well as views of cities and plans showing the layout of their streets. Munster originally wrote his text in German, which he himself translated into Latin. Soon it was translated into French, Italian, and English, which suggests how general and consistent the demand for such a book must have been. François de Belleforest added to it considerably for his Paris, 1575 version. Georg Braun, or Bruin, wrote a similar work, *Civitates orbis terrarum . . .* (Cologne, 1572–1618), with illustrations by Franz Hogenberg, showing a plan of each city and the costumes worn by the inhabitants. This collection was also translated into

123

German, and into French as *Grand Théatre des différentes cités du monde* (Brussels, 1572). A modern abridgement in English was prepared by Ruthardt Oehme, *Old European Cities* (London, 1965). Antoine du Pinet's *Plantz, pourtraictz et descriptions de plusieurs villes et forteresses tant de l'Europe, Asie, et Afrique que des Indes et Terre-Neuves* (Lyon, 1564) is the same sort of work.

5. In the *Révue du seizième siècle* for 1922 there is a photograph of an interesting sixteenth-century painting of the line of clients bearing their traditional gifts to the lawyer in his office. It is reproduced in Jean Plattard's *L'Adolescence de Rabelais en Poitou* (Paris, 1923). [LF]

6. Documentation of what follows may be found in the lively and down-to-earth *Gentilshommes campagnards de l'ancienne France*, 2d ed. (Paris, 1903), in which Pierre de Vaissière has outlined the life of rural noblemen in the sixteenth century. See also René de Maulde-la-Clavière, *Origines de la révolution française au commencement du XVIᵉ siècle* (Paris, 1889), pp. 89–106. Lucien Romier's *Le Royaume de Catherine de Médicis* (Paris, 1922) is of help for the later period. See also the documentation of chap. 9 ("La Vie du noble") of the second part of L. Febvre, *Philippe II et la Franche-Comté* (Paris, 1912). [LF]

7. The *Autobiography* of Benvenuto Cellini, trans. John Addington Symonds (New York, n.d.), II, lxxxvii. Febvre appears to be relating this incident from memory. It was necessary to pass through a great many intervening rooms to go from one end of a palace to the other in Florence and equally in most French residences of any size, as can be easily seen from their floor plans (published, for example, in Wilhelm Lübke, *Geschichte der Renaissance in Frankreich* [Stuttgart, 1885]). Montaigne, in the *Journal* of his voyage to Italy, notes that in the town of Plombières the houses are "not grand, but very comfortable since, by the use of galeries, the rooms are so arranged that they are independent of one another" (ed. Maurice Rat [Paris, n.d.], p. 9).

8. Frenchmen who expected to find rooms in winter as cold as the outside generally expressed surprise when their travels took them toward Germany and northern Italy where the common rooms of houses were heated by big ceramic stoves. Jacques-Auguste De Thou, the historian,

commented on them in 1579 when he encountered one in Mulhouse. Montaigne encountered this new form of heating in Baden, Germany, on his way to Italy in 1580. "We soaked up the warmth of their stoves to which no member of our party offered any objections. After the first moment, once an odd smell which strikes one upon entering the room has been adjusted to, the heat seems agreeable and uniform. Monsieur de Montaigne, who slept in a room with a stove and praised it highly, felt a pleasing and moderate warmth the whole night long. At least one does not burn one's face or boots, and one is freed from the smoke of France. Furthermore, whereas we take up our warm and fur-lined housecoats upon coming into the house, they, on the other hand, are in shirt-sleeves and bareheaded before the warmth of the stove, putting on additional clothing to go out-of-doors" (*Journal,* pp. 24–25).

9. François Rabelais, *The Fourth Book,* chap. 9. Febvre is paraphrasing.

10. Evidence of the importance of kitchens can be found in the numerous floor plans of sixteenth-century dwellings published by Georges Doyon and Robert Hubrecht in *L'Architecture rurale et bourgeoise en France* (Paris, 1969). Olivier de Serres (1539–1619), famous for his works on agriculture, remarked that in his day gentlemen were beginning to leave the kitchen for the sitting or dining room, a change which he felt was both snobbish and against the best interests of the landowner. He urged gentlemen to construct manor houses in which the kitchen was centrally located and used by master and servants alike, to help overcome the "natural solitude" of a country house. *Théatre de l'Agriculture et mesnage des champs* (Paris, 1615), pp. 20–22.

11. Again, the way in which people of both high and low station constructed their living places is clearly indicative of their lack of need for privacy. This is further discussed by Jean-Louis Flandrin, *Familles* (Paris, 1976), pp. 92–102.

12. See the *Propos rustiques* of Noël du Fail, chap. 6, "The Change in Sleeping between the Present and the Past." [LF] Flandrin (*Familles,* p. 97) mentions the case of Brittany where the entire household, family and servants, customarily shared a single bed. Bed was a social enough place to merit inclusion in treatises on manners intended for schoolboys:

125

"Silence becomes you in bed: talking's the thing for the court./ Also be still in your bed; just lie straight and you won't be stealing your bedfellow's clothes, tossing and turning." Giovanni Sulpitio, *Doctrina Mensae* (Oxford, 1949), p. 2, a modern translation of a fifteenth-century poem.

13. Wheat, which could not be grown at all in some mountainous areas, was always more expensive than rye, barley, oats, millet, or other grains. In times of shortage, cereal prices tended to rise more steeply than other foodstuffs, and wheat prices more steeply still. See C. Verlinden, J. Craeybeckx, E. Scholliers, "Price and Wage Movements in Belgium in the Sixteenth Century," *Economy and Society in Early Modern Europe, Essays from "Annales,"* ed. Peter Burke (New York, 1972), p. 61. Almost everywhere the government regulated the price of bread. The price of a loaf was fixed, while its weight varied with the harvests. This system (as opposed to the modern one in which the weight remains constant and the price is raised) suggests that people in the sixteenth century were much less protected from hunger. They bought their daily loaf and when the times were bad they had less to eat. In really bad times, which might happen every few years, bread was made from oats, barley, millet, peas, chestnuts, even acorns.

14. Potatoes, an import from the New World, first made their way to Europe in the sixteenth century. For the next two hundred years they were considered proper food only for animals and the desperately poor.

15. Even this was not available in regions where waterpower for running the mills which ground the flour was not available year-round (where streams froze in the winter or where they dried up in the summer). In such regions bread was stored by drying it, and later dampened enough to cut slices which were placed in the soup or in milk when it was eaten. See Marcel Arpin, *Historique de la meunerie et de la boulangerie* (Paris, 1948), pp. 244ff.

16. The central serving dish was most likely to contain a kind of vegetable soup, thickened with bread or some other starch, and flavored by a small piece of fatty meat. Precise information about the average diet in the sixteenth century, as opposed to banquet menus, is very sparse. The documents which supply us with information are such things as

the records of institutions and of taxes collected on foodstuffs; such documents are extremely difficult to interpret. Some historians have suggested that annual per capita consumption of meat was higher in the sixteenth century than in the two hundred years following. Supporting Febvre's position, B. Bennassar, for example, has computed the average annual meat consumption in Vallodolid, Spain, 1580–1590, as about forty pounds or less than a pound a week. "L'Alimentation d'une capitole espagnole au XVIe siècle," *Pour une histoire de l'alimentation,* ed. Jean-Jacques Hémardinquer (Paris, 1970), p. 53. The daily ration allotted a French sailor in the Mediterranean at about the same time is given as 1¾ pounds of bread, 1½ ounces of meat, ¾ ounce fish, 2 ounces cheese, 1½ ounces rice, 1 ounce oil, and two quarts of wine. Fresh vegetables and fruits must have been added to vary the diet and prevent scurvy (landlubbers would of course have gardens to supply them with these). The sailors' diet comes to a total of 4,000 calories, most of them bread. Michel Morineau, "Post-Scriptum: de la Hollande à la France," *Pour une histoire de l'alimentation,* p. 118. See also "Dossier: Histoire de la Consommation," ed. J. Gay and B. Bennassar, *Annales ESC,* 30 (May–June 1976), pp. 402–631, which suggests the quantity of meat may have been greater.

17. Both Fridays and Saturdays were generally meatless, as were the eves of feasts, Advent, and Lent, so that there might be 150 meatless days per year. Louis Stouff, *Ravitaillement et alimentation en Provence au XIVe et XVe siècles* (Paris, 1974), p. 234 suggests that this was the number observed in the household of the Archbishop of Arles. The consumption of eggs, milk, butter, and cheese was also forbidden on meatless days.

18. Tobacco, like the potato, came from the New World and only began to be widely used in Europe at the end of the sixteenth century. From the Middle Ages on, liqueurs and brandy were distilled, but they were thought of primarily as medicine. A late fifteenth-century text advises washing the stomach in the morning with a bit of brandy. Stouff, *Ravitaillement,* p. 251. As late as 1630 a text complains that: "Several people have been using brandy and tobacco without proper cause, for the sole purpose of satisfying

their thirst and then provoking it." Robert Mandrou, *Introduction à la France moderne, 1500–1640,* 2d ed. (Paris, 1974), p. 302; Eng. trans. by R. E. Hallmark, *Introduction to Modern France, 1500–1640: An Essay in Historical Psychology* (London, 1975). Coffee too was introduced in the sixteenth century but did not become popular until the seventeenth. Spices were used heavily in the diets of those who could afford them, but the prices given by Masson, *Les Compagnies du Corail* (Paris, 1908), p. 196, are astronomical in an age when a manual worker generally earned two to seven sous a day.

Date	Spice	Price per ounce (in sous and deniers)	Place
1520	cinnamon	1s/6d	Flanders
1520	cloves	3s/1d	Flanders
1542	pepper	7d	Soissons
1543	ginger	1s/6d	Soissons
1567	ginger	1s/3d	Marseilles
1567	pepper	1s/5d	Marseilles
1567	cloves	2s/10d	Marseilles

19. *Catalogue des Actes de François I,* 10 vols. (Paris, 1887–1908), vol. 8, "Itinéraires," p. 481 (1533). [LF]

20. Captured while besieging the Italian city of Pavia in February 1525, François I was held prisoner in Madrid for nearly a year. Pavia represented a turning point in French foreign relations; the treaties of Madrid (1525) and Cambrai (1528) which followed marked the end of French ambitions in Italy and cost France the provinces of Flanders and Artois.

21. These details and those which follow are drawn from the various accounts mentioned in the *Catalogue des Actes de François I.* Surprisingly, there is no study devoted to the court of France during this era. For the following period see M. Deloche, *Les Richelieu, Le Père du Cardinal* (Paris, 1923). François du Plessis, father of the cardinal, was appointed provost of the Hôtel and grand provost in 1578, which placed him in charge of keeping order in the royal dwelling

and its surroundings and gave him jurisdiction over the officers and servants of the royal household. M. Deloche devotes the second chapter of his book to the study of these functions, with some references to the period before 1578. [LF] The duties of the various members of the royal household are outlined in Roger Doucet, *Les Institutions de la France au XVIe siècle,* 2 vols. (Paris, 1948).

22. More information on the subject can be obtained from H. Bouchot, *Les Portraits au crayon du XVIe et XVIIe siècles conservés à la Bibliothèque Nationale* (1884); *Quelques Dames du XVIe siècle et leurs peintres* (1888) and *Les Femmes de Brantôme* (1890), these two to be taken with a grain of salt; Louis Dimier, *Histoire de la peinture de portrait en France au XVIe siècle* (Paris, Brussels, 1924), which contains a catalogue of all extant drawings and portraits of the sixteenth century. [LF] Another of Louis Dimier's books has been translated into English: *French Painting of the XVI Century* (London, 1904), of which chaps. 2, 6, and 9 are devoted to the portrait. Numerous illustrations can be found in the catalogue of the Clouet exhibition of 1970: *Les Clouet et la Cour des rois de France* (Paris, 1970).

23. Guillaume Gouffier de Bonnivet, admiral of France, was a favorite of François I. He was given both military and diplomatic assignments of the greatest importance. He advised François to attack Pavia in 1525, and during the battle in which the French lost and at which the king was taken prisoner, Bonnivet himself was killed.

24. Madame de Chateaubriand was the daughter of Gaston, Count of Foix. Her three brothers, like her father, all made considerable reputations as military men. Lautrec (Odet de Foix) was so badly wounded that he was left for dead after the battle of Ravenna in 1512. In 1521 he took Parma from the Imperial armies, only to be defeated and pushed out of Italy the following year. At Pavia he was once again wounded. While attacking Naples in 1528 he died in an epidemic that killed most of his troops as well.

25. Brantôme (Pierre de Bourdeilles, seigneur de Brantôme, 1540–1614) was the author of a collection of *Lives of Famous Men and Gallant Captains,* and *Lives of Gallant Ladies,* both, but especially the latter, collections of rather gossipy biographical anecdotes and stories of court

life, some of which he knew through his own experience. In dealing with the ladies of the court Brantôme is especially concerned with recording their amorous adventures. "Honest," in his sense, would mean being a lady or a gentleman, living according to the standards of courtly society.

26. "The mouth and the nostrils pinched, and the peculiar expression of faces long exposed to dyes and ointments, make the face displeasing and nearly absurd. The lines in the lower jaw due to age are exaggerated to form a pointy chin because the face is thin there" (Dimier, *Histoire*, p. 55). These words suffice to dissipate my scruples and clear me of any accusation of excessive severity. [LF]

27. *Relations des Ambassadeurs vénétiens sur les affaires de France au XVIᵉ siècle*, ed. Niccolò Tommaseo (Paris, 1838), I, 107–108. See, in the same vol., the report of Mario Cavelli, 1547, pp. 55–61. [LF]

28. Febvre noted in 1925 that there were no general studies of French demography available. The situation has changed, and the greatest single force of the change has been the journal of which Febvre himself was co-founder: the *Annales: Economies, Sociétés, Civilisations*. Roger Mols's *Introduction à la démographie historique des villes d'Europe du XIVᵉ au XVIIIᵉ siècle*, 3 vols. (Louvain: 1954–1956) is a basic work on the subject. A discussion of more recent work can be found in André Burguire, "La Démographie," *Faire de l'histoire*, ed. Jacques Le Goff and Pierre Nora (Paris, 1974), II, 74–104, which includes a bibliography. In English there is Robert Mandrou, *Introduction to Modern France, 1500–1640: An Essay in Historical Psychology*, trans. R. E. Hallmark (London, 1975); Peter Cox, *Demography* (Cambridge, 1970); Pierre Goubert, "Recent Theories and Research in French Population, 1500–1700," chap. 19 in *Population in History*, ed. David Victor Glass and D. E. C. Eversley (London, 1965). Louis Henry, *Anciennes Familles Genevoises* (Paris, 1956), p. 153, says that in Geneva 1550–1599, out of every 1,000 male children born, 523 died before the age of twenty. For female children the figure is 514.

29. In the *Journalier* of Jean Pussot (born 1544) we find the following entries for the year 1573, a perfectly usual year: March 3, the death of the duke of Aumale; March 18,

the birth of Pussot's second daughter; July 7, death of wife's uncle; August 27, death of eighteen-year-old wife of his brother in her fifth month of pregnancy. The year 1587 notes the death of a brother, Lenten sermons, a bad harvest, the death of both his parents, bad weather. All the events are noted without emotion, as though they were all equally important. M. Henri, ed. *Travaux de l'Académie Impériale de Reims*, 23 (1856), pp. 106–179; 25 (1856–57), pp. 1–276.

30. This scene is based on the journey recounted by Felix Platter in *Beloved Son Felix: The Journal of a Medical Student in Montpellier in the Sixteenth Century*, trans. Sean Jennet (London, 1961), pp. 32–33.

31. Children whose fathers died generally fared better than this if they had any property at all. Although the details varied from region to region, generally such a minor was placed in the joint care of two "tutors," one of whom was often his mother if she was living. The tutors were responsible for supplying all the child's needs, which were generally paid for from the estate left to the child. When he came of age, the child gained full control of whatever was left of the estate. See J. Bernard, "La Société," in *Histoire de Bordeaux*, vol. IV, *1453–1715*, ed. Robert Boutruche (Bordeaux, 1966), pp. 139–156, esp. 142–143. Extracts of tutors' accounts can be found in Charles Portal, *Extraits de régistres de notaires: Archives Historiques de l'Albigeois*, fasc. 7 (Albi, 1901), pp. 25ff; *Deux Livres de Raison: Archives Historiques de l'Albigeois*, fasc. 4, ed. Louis de Santi and August Vidal (Paris, 1896), pp. 45ff.

32. Thomas Platter, *Lebensbeschreibung*, ed. Alfred Hartmann (Klosterberg Basle, 1944). There is an English translation by Paul Monroe, *Thomas Platter and the Educational Renaissance of the Sixteenth Century* (New York, 1904).

33. "De Votis temere susceptis [Rash Vows]," *The Colloquies of Erasmus*, trans. Craig R. Thompson (Chicago, 1965), p. 6.

2. THE QUEST FOR KNOWLEDGE

1. Whether there were renaissances before the Renaissance, the degree to which the Renaissance was a singular development, the degree of continuity or discontinuity between the Renaissance and the Middle Ages have been,

and to some extent remain, contested issues. See Charles Homer Haskins, *The Renaissance of the Twelfth Century* (Cambridge, Mass., 1927), reprinted as a Meridian Paperback, 1957; Wallace K. Ferguson, *The Renaissance in Historical Thought: Five Centuries of Interpretation* (Cambridge, Mass., 1948); Peter Burke, *The Renaissance Sense of the Past* (London, 1969), how the Renaissance saw itself; Franco Simone, *The French Renaissance: Medieval Tradition and Italian Influence in Shaping the Renaissance in France*, trans. H. Gaston Hall (London, 1969; Italian ed., 1961); Erwin Panofsky, *Renaissance and Renascences* (Stockholm, 1965), primary emphasis on the visual arts and on Italy.

2. *Pierre Viret d'après lui-même: Pages extraites des oeuvres du Réformateur à l'occasion du quatrième centenaire de sa naissance*, ed. Charles Schetzler, Henri Vuilleumier, Alfred Schröder (Lausanne, 1911), p. 4. [LF]

3. This remark is taken from the sometimes odd but often useful book by René de Maulde-la-Clavière, *Les Origines de la révolution française au commencement du XVIᵉ siècle: la veille de la réforme* (Paris, 1889), p. 3. [LF] The combination of security and prestige seems to have been maintained in the first part of the century by focusing Frenchmen's fighting energies toward Italy, contributing thus to peace at home and prestige gained from victories abroad.

4. Each of these battles marked a major victory in the wars conducted by Charles VIII, Louis XII, and François I to control various parts of Italy which they had more or less good reasons for believing to be rightfully theirs: the Duchy of Milan and the Kingdom of Naples, primarily. In 1495 Charles VIII conquered Naples. The other Italian states formed a league to prevent the balance of power in Italy from being drastically altered, and, at the battle of Fornovo, attempted to block the homeward path of the French. Fornovo was a decisive French victory.

In 1498 Louis XII and his armies led by Gian-Giacopo Trivulzio, conquered Milan, to which Louis had a claim dating from the early fifteenth century. Two years later the former ruler of Milan, Ludovico il Moro Sforza, led an uprising against the French which was put down at the battle of Novarra, where the French general Louis II de la Tremoille took Ludovico prisoner. Next the Genoese came under direct French rule. In 1509 Louis XII himself led the French forces to victory over the Venetians at Agnadello, a victory which brought great prestige but little advancement to the French claims in Italy. Much the same can be said for Ravenna in 1512, although the victory of the French forces led by Gaston de Foix did cost the pope control of the Romagna. François I, not to be left out, launched an attack intended to reconquer Milan as soon as he became king in 1515. His victory at Marignano not only returned Milan to French control but won the respect of all Europe for France's military prowess.

5. All four men were great military leaders during the Italian campaigns. Louis II de la Tremoille, viscount of Thouars and prince of Talmont (1487–1525), started his distinguished military career at the age of twenty-seven, leading the French against the Duke of Brittany. He died at the battle of Pavia. Gaston de Foix, Duke of Nemours (1489–1512), nephew of King Louis XII, had demonstrated considerable brilliance as a military strategist before his premature death following the battle of Ravenna. Gian-Giacopo Trivulzio (1447–1518) came from a distinguished military family. He was chief adviser to the young Gaston de Foix. Taking over his command at his death Trivulzio played a major part in the French victory at Marignano, but died in disgrace after having lost the siege of Brescia. Bayard, properly, Pierre du Terrail, sieur of Bayard (1473–1523), was perhaps the best known soldier of his time. He served under Charles VIII, Louis XII, and François I. Single-handedly, he held back a troop of two hundred Spaniards at the bridge of Garigliano. His exploits were the subject of two contemporary biographies, one of which has been translated: Jacques Mailles, *The Very Joyous, Pleasant, and Refreshing History of the Feats, Exploits, Triumphs, and Achievements of the Good Knight without Fear and without Reproach, the Gentle Lord de Bayard*, trans. Edward Cockburn Kindersley (London, 1845).

6. The devastation produced by war, plague, and general disorder was such that many towns disappeared entirely. The land returned to a wild state and had to be cleared again and new boundaries marked. For example one town south of Paris was left with six standing houses, seven

houses with walls alone, and forty-five foundations. Yvonne Bézard, *La Vie rurale dans le sud de la région parisiènne, 1450–1550* (Paris, 1929), p. 47. For more information on taxation and related matters in the reign of Louis XI see *The Recovery of France in the Fifteenth Century*, ed. P. S. Lewis, trans. G. F. Martin (London, 1971).

7. General information on the economic renaissance is in Pierre Imbart de la Tour, *Les Origines de la Réforme* (Paris, 1905), vol. I. [LF] See also Fernand Braudel, *The Mediterranean and the Mediterranean World in the Age of Philip II*, trans. Siân Reynolds (New York, 1973), II, 893ff.

8. Eng. trans., Stanford, Calif., 1953. See also Febvre's article: "Les Nouveaux-riches et l'histoire," *Revue des Cours et Conférences*, 25, 2d ser. (15 June 1922), pp. 423–440. [LF]

9. See Lucien Febvre, *Philippe II et la Franche-Comté* (Paris, 1912), book 2, chap. 10. [LF] Reprinted 1970.

10. On the beginnings of printing in France see H. Omont, "La Bibliothèque du roi au début du règne de Louis XV," *Mémoires de la société de l'histoire de Paris*, 20 (1892), pp. 207–294. [LF] Since then several useful books on the subject have appeared: Ernst Goldschmidt, *Medieval Texts and Their First Appearance in Print* (London, 1943); Curt F. Bühler, *The Fifteenth Century Book* (Philadelphia, 1960) discusses the slow process by which people began to make the modern radical distinction between manuscripts and printed books; Lucien Febvre and Henri-Jean Martin, *The Coming of the Book: The Impact of Printing in Western Europe, 1450–1800* (Atlantic Highlands, N.J., 1976; French ed., 1958); Rudolph Hirsch, *Printing, Selling, and Reading, 1450–1550* (Wiesbaden, 1967).

11. The *Distiches* of Cato (*Disticha* Catonis), a postclassical Roman, were used as a textbook throughout the Middle Ages. The combination they offered of easy Latin and laudable moral sentiments assured their popularity. Aelius Donatus wrote his elementary Latin grammar in the fourth century A.D. and it too was replaced as a schoolbook only in the mid-sixteenth century. *De Moribus in Mensa Servandis* (On Table Manners) is a verse treatise of 120 lines on manners in general, composed by Johannes Sulpitius (died about 1440), first printed in 1483 and often thereafter. Frequently it was included in the same volume as elementary

Latin texts (for example, the *Auctores Octo*) for the purpose of teaching manners and Latin at the same time. It has been reprinted twice in modern times: Giovanni Sulpizio of Veroli, *Doctrina Mensae*, facsimile of 1510 Seville edition, with an English verse translation, introduction, and notes by Henry Thomas (Oxford, 1949) and *Table Manners for Boys*, Latin Manuscript by a Pseudo-Ovid (London, 1958), under the auspices of the Wine and Food Society. The variations of the title of this treatise are not at all uncommon in fifteenth- and early sixteenth-century books; only when printing made larger collections of books a common occurrence did titles begin to have some importance.

12. This is illustrated in Augustin Renaudet's excellent book, *Préréforme et humanisme en France pendant les premières guerres d'Italie* (Paris, 1916). [LF] Reprinted 1953. The effect of printing on ordinary people, tradesmen and the like, is discussed by Natalie Zenon Davis, "Printing and the People," *Society and Culture in Early Modern France* (Stanford, Calif. 1975), pp. 189–226.

13. This fascination with death in the fifteenth century is discussed in Jan Huizinga's classic *Waning of the Middle Ages* (New York, n.d.; Original Dutch ed. 1924), especially chap. 9.

14. The *Imitation of Christ*, attributed to the fifteenth-century Dutchman Thomas à Kempis, recommended that the pious Christian should model his own life on that of Christ in both practical and mystical ways. It was hugely popular through the sixteenth century in the original Latin and in translation. For more information about this work see Albert Hyma, *The Christian Renaissance: A History of the "Devotio Moderna,"* 2d ed. (Hamden, Conn., 1965), pp. 158ff.

15. François Rabelais, *Gargantua*, especially chap. 15.

16. In 1476 George Hieronymus taught Greek in Paris. His competence was questioned by his students, who included such future luminaries of the world of learning as Erasmus, Budé, and Reuchlin. Twenty years later Jean Lascaris, a serious scholar, taught Greek in Paris once again. Lascaris' Greek grammar, published by Aldus in Venice, 1495, was the first serious Greek grammar available to students of the language. From 1508 to 1512 Jerome

Aleander was charged with teaching Greek in the French capital. As these dates suggest, there were more years in which no one could teach Greek during this period than years with even so incompetent a source as Hieronymus. For more information see John Edwin Sandys, *A History of Classical Scholarship,* vol. 2, *From the Revival of Learning to the End of the Eighteenth Century* (Cambridge, 1909); R. R. Bolgar, *The Classical Heritage and Its Beneficiaries* (Cambridge, Eng., 1953, 1973).

17. The books of Thomas Platter's two sons have been translated into English: *Beloved Son Felix: The Journal of Felix Platter, a Medical Student in Montpellier in the Sixteenth Century,* trans. Sean Jennet (London, 1961); *The Journal of a Younger Brother: The Life of Thomas Platter as a Medical Student in Montpellier at the Close of the Sixteenth Century,* trans. Sean Jennet (London, 1963). For the autobiography of Thomas Platter, Sr., see essay 1, note 32, above.

18. The Valais is a mountainous canton in southwestern Switzerland.

19. Sebastion Castellion (or Castellio, or Chateillon, 1515–1563) was the first person to propose a theory of religious toleration in his book *De Hereticis an sit Persequendi* (1554); Eng. trans. by Roland S. Bainton, *Concering Heretics, Whether They are to be Persecuted and How they are to be Treated* (New York, 1935). In addition to his works on tolerance and his translation of the Bible, he wrote Latin dialogues based on the Bible for use in Protestant schools. Like Platter, Castellion had a distinguished career as a schoolmaster. For further information see Roland S. Bainton, "Sebastion Castellion, Champion of Liberty," *Castellioniana* (Leiden, 1951), pp. 25–79; includes bibliography.

20. This may have been Du Chastel. See Robert Doucet, "P. Du Chastel, grand aumonier de la France," *Revue historique,* 134 (Jan.–April 1920), pp. 212–257; (May–Aug. 1920), pp. 1–57. [LF] Du Chastel followed Erasmus to Basle. He returned to France to become Bishop of Orléans and grand aumonier (chief ecclesiastical officer of the court) to François Í. He remained a stout defender of evangelicals all his life.

21. See Augustin Renaudet, "Jean Standonck, un réformateur catholique avant la réforme," *Bulletin de la société de*

l'histoire du Protestanisme, 56 (Jan.–Feb. 1908), pp. 1–81. [LF] Reprinted in A. Renaudet, *Humanisme et Renaissance* (Geneva, 1958), pp. 114–161. On Standonck in English see Albert Hyma, *The Christian Renaissance*, 2d ed. (Hamden, Conn., 1965), pp. 236ff. The same chapter, with minor variations, appears in Albert Hyma, *Renaissance to Reformation* (Grand Rapids, Mich., 1951), pp. 337ff. Standonck became principal of the Collège de Montaigu in Paris.

22. François Rabelais, *Gargantua*, chap. 37.

23. Henri de Mesmes, *Mémoires inédits*, ed. Edouard Fremy (Paris, 1886; reprinted Geneva, 1970), pp. 138—140. Looking back, Mesmes himself suggests that this schedule was more than might be expected of a boy.

24. Felix Platter, *Beloved Son Felix*, p. 127.

25. This was a common and widespread belief in France. See Jobbé Duval, *Les Idées primitives dans la Bretagne contemporaine* (Paris, 1920). [LF]

26. Henri Busson, *Les Sources et le développement du rationalisme de la littérature française de la Renaissance* (Paris, 1922), book 1, chap. 1, is devoted to these authors and their influence on the thought of the sixteenth century. [LF]

27. This interest in Africa and the eastern Mediterranean on the part of the peoples of the western Mediterranean is discussed by Fernand Braudel, *The Mediterranean and the Mediterranean World in the Age of Philip II*, trans. Siân Reynolds, 2 vols. (New York, 1972), I, 134ff. Venetian trade with the East, pp. 388ff, 548ff, was the framework for much of the contact between West and East.

28. An excellent example of one of these adventurers on the road to knowledge can be found in the life of Pierre Belon, as recounted by Paul Delaunay in the *Revue du seizième siècle*, 9 (1922), pp. 251–268; 10 (1923), pp. 1–34; 11 (1924), pp. 30–48 and 222–232; 12 (1925), pp. 78–98 and 256–283. [LF] Published in book form: *L'Aventureuse existence de Pierre Belon du Mans* (Paris, 1926).

29. Vesalius' book *On the Structure of the Human Body* probably was first printed in 1538, and then again in Basle by Oporinus in 1543.

30. See the maps accompanying vol. 2 of the *Bibliotheca Bio-bibliografica della Terra Santa e del Oriente Francescano*, by Girolamo Golubovitch (Karachi, 1913). [LF]

3. THE QUEST FOR BEAUTY

1. Leonardo was in France from 1516 to his death in 1519. The great goldsmith Benvenuto Cellini worked for François I from 1540 to 1545. Francesco Primaticcio came in 1532 and stayed until his death in 1570. Some discussion and reproductions of the works of all three executed for the French court can be found in Desmond Seward, *Prince of the Renaissance: The Life of François I* (London, 1973).

2. A survey of the artistic centers in France during the fifteenth century can be found in Louis Réau, *French Painting in the XIV, XV, and XVI Century,* trans. Mary Chamot (London, 1939), which includes biographies of the painters as well as many reproductions in black and white and some in dubious color.

3. The story, reported by Vasari among others, is that Antonello learned to paint in oil from van Eyck and then passed his new knowledge on to other Italians, particularly to Bellini. Until then the Italians painted in tempera. The advantage of oil as a medium for holding the color is that it is itself transparent (unlike egg yolk, the medium for tempera) and permits the development of techniques which use multiple layers of transparent glazes so that light seems to be held and to come from the painting itself. Oil therefore represents a major technical advance.

4. Jean, Duke of Berry (died 1416), youngest brother of King Charles V of France, spent the greater part of his energy and his wealth in the acquisition of works of art of all kinds. The collection was dispersed at his death to pay his debts, and he is most remembered for the numerous exquisitely illustrated Books of Hours he commissioned. René de Provence (1409–1480) was, at one point, Count of Anjou and Provence, Duke of Lorraine, and King of Naples and Sicily. Through various misfortunes, he lost everything but the county of Provence, where he ended his days much beloved by his subjects. He was not only an active patron of the arts, he himself composed poetry and painted. Philippe le Bon (1396–1467), Duke of Burgundy, held one of the most magnificent courts in the Europe of his day. Burgundy under his reign became the greatest artistic center in the French-speaking world.

5. Charles the Bold, Duke of Burgundy, was a French

noble in that his ancestor, Philippe, with whom the new dynasty of Dukes of Burgundy began, was the son of French King Jean II. Many Burgundian nobles had family connections with French nobility, and commoners too had ties, not only of consanguinity but also of common custom and language.

6. For examples of the work of Sluter and the Burgundian school of sculpture see Theodor Müller, *Sculpture in the Netherlands, Germany, France, and Spain 1400–1500,* trans. Elaine and William Robson Scott (Baltimore, 1966), pp. 7–14, pls. 1–15.

7. For examples of the work of Stephan Lochner and of the Cologne school see Renzo Chiarelli, Margherita Lenzini Moriondo, and Franco Mazzini, *European Painting in the Fifteenth Century,* trans. H. E. Scott (New York, 1961), pp. 29 and 235.

8. For examples of the work of the school of Avignon see *European Painting,* pp. 211, 216, 217, and Jacques Lassaigne and Giulio Carlo Argan, *The Fifteenth Century from Van Eyck to Botticelli,* trans. Stuart Gilbert (New York, n.d.), pp. 71–73, 181–184.

9. The *Très Riches Heures* was an illustrated prayer book designed to be used in private devotions. Such a book, very popular in the fifteenth century, is called a Book of Hours. The choice of prayers varies somewhat, but usually includes the Offices of the Virgin, the psalms, litanies, and the Offices of the dead. There are nearly always illustrations depicting, for example, an event in the life of the Virgin to coincide with each of the eight times of the day when the eight prayers of her Office were to be said. Generally the illustrations also include a Calendar, twelve scenes, showing an occupation suited to each month (hay making in July, hunting in November). Numerous reproductions of some of the miniatures have been published—the Calendar, for example, presented by Jean Porcher, *Les Très Riches Heures du duc de Berry* (Paris, n.d.). A single example is included in *European Painting,* p. 18. See also Erwin Panofsky, *Early Netherlandish Painting* (Cambridge, Mass., 1958), II, figs. 80–84, 87–91, 93, 95 (b&w). Even with modern technology, a reproduction is but a pale echo of the real thing.

10. Emile Mâle, *The Gothic Image: Religious Art in France*

of the Thirteenth Century, trans. Dora Nussey (New York, 1958; orig. Eng. trans., 1913).

11. A discussion of this change can be found in Max Dvorak, *Idealism and Naturalism in Gothic Art,* trans. Randolph J. Klawiter (Notre Dame, Ind., 1967; 1st German ed., 1918).

12. The first two of these examples, all of which are sculptures, are among the photographs included in Mâle's book, figs. 16 and 141 respectively.

13. A similar Annunciation by the Master of Flémalle (although without the Saint Christopher, unfortunately) can be found in *Early Netherlandish Painting,* II, fig. 204 (b&w).

14. See *The Fifteenth Century,* p. 153; *Early Netherlandish,* II, figs. 462–463.

15. For examples of Fouquet's painting see *European Painting,* pp. 213–214; *The Fifteenth Century,* pp. 74–80.

16. Ghirlandaio's *Adoration of the Shepherds* is reproduced by Ernst Steinmann, *Ghirlandaio* (Leipzig, 1897), p. 33 (b&w).

17. A full discussion of this famous painting, a black and white reproduction, many details, and copies by painters who saw it in better condition can be found in Ludwig, H. Heydenreich, *Leonardo: The Last Supper* (New York, 1974).

18. "Quatre Entretiens sur la Peinture," *Les Arts en Portugal,* trans. Comte A. Raczsynski (Paris, 1946) [LF], p. 14.

19. The correspondence of Albrecht Dürer provides some insight into the relations between Northern and Italian art. From Venice in 1506 Dürer wrote home: "Amongst the Italians I have many good friends who warn me not to eat and drink with their painters. Many of them are my enemies and they copy my work in the churches and wherever they find it; and then they revile it and say that it was not in the *antique* manner and therefore not good. Giovanni Bellini, however, has highly praised me before many nobles." *A Documentary History of Art,* vol. 1, *The Middle Ages and the Renaissance,* ed. Elizabeth G. Holt (New York, 1957), pp. 330–331.

20. At the Hospice of Saint John as well as at Saint Bavo's cathedral the present-day curators have a large magnifying glass available to lend any visitor. Reproductions of a part of

the *Adoration of the Mystic Lamb* (the Ghent Altarpiece), the Van Eyck painting in Saint Bavo's, can be found in *European Painting,* p. 190 and the *Fifteenth Century,* p. 17. The whole painting is reproduced in *Early Netherlandish,* II, figs. 274–283 (b&w).

21. This new conception of the artist is a recurrent subject in Anthony Blunt, *Artistic Theory in Italy, 1450–1600* (Oxford, 1940), especially chap. 4, "The Social Position of the Artist."

22. This is a quotation from a letter Dürer wrote from Venice in 1506. The letter is included in Wolfgang Stechow, *Northern Renaissance Art, 1400–1600: Sources and Documents* (Englewood Cliffs, N.J., 1966). The form Stechow gives is: "Here I am a gentleman, at home only a parasite" (p. 91).

23. See Jean Plattard, *L'Adolescence de Rabelais en Poitou* (Paris, 1923), pp. 11ff. [LF] Anthony Blunt, *Philibert de l'Orme* (London, 1958), pp. 8–14, sees the influence of Philibert on the plans of the Abbey of Theleme.

24. Vitruvius' *Eight Books on Architecture* were not translated into French until 1547 by Jean Martin (who, two years earlier, translated Serlio's *Six Books on Architecture*). Naturally, Vitruvius was read in France before this, either in Latin or in one of the annotated Italian translations. [LF] Vitruvius' work was a record of Roman architectural theory and practice in about 80 B.C. Leon Battista Alberti (1404–1472), *De Re Aedificatoria,* was a kind of Renaissance continuation of Vitruvius. See Joan Gadol, *Leon Battista Alberti, Universal Man of the Early Renaissance* (Chicago, 1969), especially pp. 117ff.

25. On the relations between Rabelais and Philandrier see Arthur Heulhard, *Rabelais, Ses voyages en Italie, son exil à Metz* (Paris, 1891), pp. 274ff. [LF]

26. Examples cited by Lazare Sainéan, *La Langue de Rabelais* (Paris, 1922), I, 54–55, suggest that the words *architecture* and *architecte* first appeared in French in 1539–1546. [LF] Huguet's *Dictionaire de la langue française du seizième siècle* finds the words used by Jean Lemaire de Belges (before 1514) and Geoffroy Tory, *Champfleury* (1529), but in these earlier uses the primary application is not buildings but the idea of construction—for example, God is called the *architecteur de la machine ronde* (constructor of the globe).

27. There are some interesting remarks on this subject in Jacques Mesnil, *L'Art au nord et au sud des Alpes,* especially pp. 57ff. [LF] Quattrocento inquiries into perspective and the results are discussed by Gadol, *Leon Battista Alberti,* pp. 21ff and Samuel Y. Edgerton, Jr., *The Renaissance Discovery of Linear Perspective* (New York, 1975). Selections from the writings of Alberti, Piero della Francesca, and Leonardo are in Elizabeth G. Holt, *A Documentary History of Art* (New York, 1957; 1st ed., 1947), pp. 203ff, 253ff, and 279ff; on anatomical progress see pp. 286ff (Leonardo).

28. Mantegna's Christ is in the Brera Gallery in Milan. A reproduction can be found in Lionello Venturi and Rosabianca Skira-Venturi, *The Creators of the Renaissance,* trans. Stuart Gilbert (Geneva, 1950), I, 157.

29. On the subject see Louis Dimier, *Le Primatice* (Paris, 1900) [LF]. Primaticcio (see the first note to this essay) was the Italian painter responsible for much of the decoration of François I's chateau at Fontainebleau. The chateau became the center for the growth of Italianate art in France, hence we speak of the school of Fontainebleau. See also Seward, *Prince of the Renaissance.* There are many reproductions in the catalogue of the 1972 exposition at the Grand Palais, *L'Ecole de Fontainebleau* (Paris, 1972).

30. The development of French architecture is masterfully exposed in Louis Hautecoeur's *Histoire de l'architecture classique en France,* vol. 1, *La Formation de l'idéal classique,* part 1, *La Première Renaissance, 1495–1540* (Paris, 1963); part 2, *La Renaissance des Humanistes, 1540–1589* (Paris, 1965).

31. See Louis Dimier, *French Painting in the Sixteenth Century* (London, 1904), pp. 6ff; for Corneille de Lyon, pp. 127ff; for Italianism in the reign of Henri III, pp. 145ff. [LF] See also Peter Mellen, *Jean Clouet* (London, 1971), which has a complete catalogue of the extant works of Clouet.

4. THE QUEST FOR GOD

1. On Luther's trip to Rome see H. Böhmer, *Luthers Romfahrt* (Leipzig, 1914) and Otto Scheel's biography, *Martin Luther,* vol. 2, *Im Kloster* (Tübingen, 1917). [LF] In English there is Heinrich Böhmer, *Luther in the Light of Recent Research,* trans. Carl F. Huth, Jr. (New York, 1916) and by the

same author, *Road to Reformation,* trans. John W. Doberstein and Theo G. Tappert (Philadelphia, 1946). Also Lucien Febvre, *Martin Luther, a Destiny,* trans. Roberts Tapley (New York, 1929), what Febvre himself calls a psychological biography, examines the process by which Luther found himself committed to beliefs which made necessary his break with the Church of Rome.

2. *Histoire de France:* book 2, chap. 7, *"La Renaissance."* [LF]

3. Useful information on this subject can be found in René de Maulde-la-Clavière, *Les Origines de la révolution française au commencement du seizième siècle* (Paris, 1889), pp. 159ff. [LF] See also Gabriel Le Bras, *L'Eglise et le village* (Paris, 1976) for information on this and other topics concerning the church and the rural faithful.

4. Such sermons were usually well attended; they were considered as much an entertainment as a religious function. In Paris preachers came into and fell out of fashion, like popular singers. Either the texts or the outlines of the sermons of successful and respected preachers (Jean Gerson, Michel Menot, Olivier Maillard) were published for the use of others with less skill, learning, or imagination.

5. Emile Longin, "Le Manuscrit de Jacques Cordelier de Clairvaux (1570–1637)," *Mémoires de la société d'émulation du Jura,* 6th ser., vol. 3 (1898), pp. 248–284. [LF] The quotation is from pp. 283–284.

6. Jules Michelet, *Histoire de France,* "Introduction à la Renaissance." [LF]

7. See Augustin Renaudet's fine book *Préréforme et humanisme à Paris pendant les premières guerres d'Italie* (Paris, 1916), pp. 61ff especially for Ockhamism. [LF] There is a discussion of the philosophical ideas of Ockham and his followers in Frederick Copleston, *A History of Philosophy,* vol. 3, part 1, *Ockham to the Speculative Mystics* (New York, 1953), pp. 56–133. On the split between the common people and the "intellectuals," and on the state of the church in general during this period, see Paul Ourliac and Henri Gilles, *Histoire du Droit et des institutions de l'église en occident,* vol 13, *La Periode post-classique, 1378–1500* (Paris, 1971).

Ockham was an English Franciscan (ca. 1290–1349).

Ockhamism as a system is roughly synonomous with *via moderna,* terminism, or simply nominalism. What characterizes all such systems is a belief that general terms—for example, cat—stand for individual things alone—for example, my cat, the cat in the alley—and that the idea "cat," the universal, is merely a convenience of language. Ockhamists also believed in the "principle of contradiction," that is, that only statements whose opposite creates no contradiction are absolutely certain. This permits very few certainties. (For example: My cat is black. All cats which are not my cat are not black. As the second statement is false, the first is not certain.) The exclusion of certainty from many areas of philosophical inquiry, such as the existence of God, which Ockham denied could be certain, made faith an absolute quality, unbuttressed by the efforts of reason. This stance had some appeal for mystics, who often had little use for reason in the first place. The application to theology of the extreme nominalism advocated by the Ockhamist resulted in a clear gulf between theology and philosophy, since man could not come in contact with universals, which existed in name only in this world, and universals are the manner in which God is manifest. God is therefore unknowable for man, and accessible only by faith.

8. See Renaudet, *Préréforme,* as well, for the full light he sheds on the numerous attempts at monastic reform which took place in France in the early sixteenth century. [LF] There were efforts, for example, to reform monasteries according to the rules of the Windesheim congregations, rules which included poverty, silence, and consultation between the abbot or father superior and the monks before making decisions which would affect them all. The attraction of the cloistered life at just this time is suggested by the example of Lefebvre d'Etaples, a leading figure in the evangelical movement, what Renaudet calls *préréforme,* who quite seriously considered becoming a monk in 1491, when he was already forty years old (Renaudet, p. 204). On the Windesheim reform movement see Albert Hyma, *The Christian Renaissance* (Hamden, Conn., 1965), pp. 137ff, especially pp. 152–157.

9. Many people felt the need for reform in the Church

and for a return to the text of the bible as a guide for the faithful. They worked for change within the Church. Luther, when asked to choose between his personal beliefs and the dicta of the Church, chose his own faith. That decision, a conscious, voluntary break, marks the start of the Reformation.

10. Marguerite de Navarre (1492–1549) wrote several collections of mystical religious verse (in addition to secular works). Her religious feelings were also expressed in more active ways; her court (she was Queen of Navarre) was a haven for those hounded by the theologians. Febvre examined her religious attitudes—and the alternatives available in France in the second quarter of the sixteenth century—in *Amour sacré, amour profane. Autour de l'Heptaméron* (Paris, 1944).

11. This is true not only in churches but in homes as well. Among the artworks described by inventories of ordinary homes in the rural area just south of Paris, 1450–1550, there is a distinct preference for images of suffering, the Virgin of mercy, Saint Sebastian, the passion of Christ. See Yvonne Bézard, *La Vie rurale au sud de la région parisienne, 1450–1550* (Paris, 1929), p. 304.

12. The donors of these fifteenth-century chapels in Bourges cathedral—chapels in which they and their families could have mass said, could commemorate a patron saint in the stained-glass window, or could be buried when they died—were the cream of the bourgeoisie of the region. For example, Jacques Coeur (died 1461), was the richest man in France, possibly in all Europe. He was born the son of a goldsmith and rose to become comptroller (and provider) of the king's finances under Charles VII. Simon Aligret (died 1415) was personal physician to the Duc de Berry (of *Très Riches Heures* fame) and amassed a considerable fortune largely due to the duke's generosity. His chapel, especially the magnificent windows, is perhaps the most admired aesthetically. Pierre Tullier (died 1532) was a lawyer, king's counsel, and mayor of Bourges (1479–1482); his brothers and nephews chose careers within the church and became canons.

13. Frère Jean is the friar in Rabelais' *Gargantua* who be-

lieves in the merits of action (chaps. 39ff). He reappears in *The Fourth Book* as the advocate of practical action by man (chaps. 19–22).

14. The Fugger family, engaged in commerce since the start of the fifteenth century, bloomed under the leadership of Jacob Fugger, known as Jacob the Rich, in the last quarter of the century. They had major business interests in northern and central Europe, as well as Italy, Spain, and the New World. Pierre Janin, *Merchants of the 16th Century,* trans. Paul Fittingoff (New York, 1972; French ed., 1969) speaks of the century following Jacob the Rich as the Age of the Fuggers (roughly 1475–1575). Money was as important in elections then as it is now, and since both the emperor and the pope were elected, the Fuggers came to have a large say in the matter.

15. The source of this anecdote is *Documents inédits sur la réformation dans le pays de Neuchâtel,* ed. Arthur Piaget (Neuchâtel, 1909), doc. 52, pp. 134ff. [LF]

16. Janotus de Bragmardo appears in Rabelais' *Gargantua* (chap. 19) as a representative of the theologians of the University of Paris who makes a very pompous, highfalutin, formalist, and empty speech requesting that Gargantua, who is a giant, return the university's bells which he had taken from the belfry.

Thubal Holofernes (Thubal means worldly confusion in Hebrew; Holofernes suggests the ferocious tyrant of the biblical *Book of Judith,* who is taken as a type of the persecutor of the Church) also appears in *Gargantua* (chap. 14). Holofernes is appointed tutor to the young Gargantua, who memorizes many useless things until his tutor dies of the pox.

17. Michael Servetus, a Spanish physician burned at the stake in Geneva in 1553, was the first heretic to die in Protestant hands. Servetus had unorthodox views on the Trinity and infant baptism, either of which would have been enough to have him sent to the flames by the Catholic Inquisition. That would very likely have been his fate if Calvin had not caught him on his way through Geneva. See Roland H. Bainton, *Hunted Heretic: The Life and Death of Michael Servetus, 1511–1553* (Boston, 1953). Berthelier's death was more the victory of Calvin's political ideas than his religious ones.

18. The first theoretical work on tolerance was, in fact, written in direct response to the burning of Servetus. Sebastion Castellion's *Treatise of Heretics* was published within months of Servetus' death. For more on the development of ideas of tolerance in the sixteenth century see Roland H. Bainton, Bruno Becker, Marius Valkhoff, Sape van der Woude, *Castellioniana* (Leiden, 1951); Joseph Lecler, *Toleration and Reformation,* trans, T. L. Westow (New York, 1960).

19. Melanchthon (1497–1560) was perhaps Luther's (1483–1546) closest disciple; although he shared Luther's beliefs, he was, by inclination and by training, much more intellectual than Luther. Beza (Theodore de Beze, 1519–1605) had a very similar position with respect to Calvin (1509–1564). Both men became leaders of the second generation, so to speak, of the Reform.

20. The process of moving from a position of no political power and a strong theoretical defense of liberty of conscience to increasing power accompanied by acceptance of restraints on personal liberty of conscience is traced in Febvre's *Martin Luther, a Destiny.* Calvin's position was simpler. He believed that people had a right to believe the truth, and he always knew himself to be in possession of that Truth. Catholic truth might be tolerated out of pragmatism. Bainton goes so far as to suggest that if Calvin ever wrote anything in favor of toleration it was probably a printer's error.

21. Pierre-Josephe Proudhon, *La Révolution sociale démontrée par le coup d'état du deux décembre* (Paris, 1852), pp. 46–47. [LF]

5. The Renaissance Merchant

1. For the early history of the French postal service see Eugene Vaillé, *Histoire générale des postes françaises,* vol. 2 (Paris, 1949). Postal service was originally limited to government business, but this clearly was never very well enforced, and as the sixteenth century wore on the restriction was abandoned. Universities as well as cities established more or less regular messenger service between certain points. For example, the University of Paris offered a weekly run to Rouen. In the early days of the royal postal

service, routes were not fixed; they followed the movements of the court and the press of events. Postal riders changed horses about every twenty miles, which meant assuring that there would be a source of fresh horses for the royal couriers. This improved conditions for other messenger services and for travelers in general.

2. In the last quarter of the sixteenth century there was regular biweekly service between Lyon and Madrid, with the departing messenger for Madrid leaving two days before the arriving messenger appeared, so that all responses were delayed twelve days.

3. In spite of these conditions, trade depended upon the mails, as is suggested by the huge volume of mail in merchants' archives. A substantial trading firm in Nantes received in a single year, 1579, some 2,620 letters sent from other parts of France, and Spain, Portugal, the Netherlands, Germany, and Italy. See Henri Lapeyre, *Une Famille de marchands, les Ruiz* (Paris, 1955), p. 159.

4. While the establishment of roads may have meant some improvement in travel conditions, it had other consequences as well. When all roads were equally abominable the traveler, often a merchant, chose his route according to the chances of having traveling companions, or finding a better inn at day's end, or rumors of deals to be made along the way. Many towns therefore had shared the traffic which was now channeled to only one town by the post roads. On alternate routes see Braudel, *The Mediterranean* (London, 1972), I, 217; Emil Coornaert, *Les Français et le commerce international à Anvers* (Paris, 1961), II, 181ff, 208.

5. These are some of the names given to Roman roads in various parts of France. Guillaume Paradin, *Histoire de Lyon* (Lyon, 1573; reprinted Roanne, 1973), p. 89, explains that the wife of King Sigebert of Austrasie, Brunehaut (534–613), ordered extensive repairs to the Roman road system of raised, paved roads broad enough for two carts abreast. These roads were still in use in Paradin's day, when, in fact, the Roman roads were probably the only roads outside of towns which were paved, and the only roads which were that wide. See Olwen Brogan, *Roman Gaul* (London, 1953), pp. 28–37. For illustrations see Hans Hitzer, *Die Strasse* (Munich, 1971), pl. 139.

6. Charles Estienne, in his 1553 guide for travelers, *La Guide des Chemins de France,* ed. Jean Bonnerot (Paris, 1936) repeatedly refers to stretches of road as "rue d'enfer," hell street. Fords are by far the most frequent way across rivers mentioned in the guide, and are often noted as bad or dangerous. Febvre discusses these problems in *Philippe II et la Franche-Comté* (Paris, 1912, 1970), chap. 8, sec. 3.

7. Robbery on the roads, mentioned also in essay 1, above, is frequently a theme of illustrations. See Hitzer, *Die Strasse,* pls. 182 (sharing the loot), 197, 199 (an attack in the woods), 200.

8. In Febvre's example the cost of transport was 2.5 percent for a relatively short time and a short distance. This was neither exorbitant nor unusual. Martin Wolfe, *The Fiscal System of Renaissance France* (New Haven, 1972), p. 112, mentions a sum of 125,000 livres for which the transport costs were 6,750 livres, or 5.4 percent of the total.

9. Bales of leather were another, and perhaps safer, means of hiding money. Braudel, *The Mediterranean,* I, 478, suggests that as much as 400,000 ducats worth of gold coins may have been smuggled this way in the 1560s alone. A photograph of a trunk for carrying currency can be found in Hitzer, *Die Strasse,* pl. 173.

10. The sons of François I, left hostage in Madrid in place of their father (see essay 1, note 20, above), were ransomed for four million livres. The first payment, about half the total sum, required a thirty-two mule pack train. See also Braudel, *The Mediterranean,* I, 484–485.

11. Marc Brésard, *Les Foires de Lyon aux XVe et XVIe siècles* (Paris, 1914). [LF] Coornaert, *Les Français et le commerce international à Anvers,* II, 140, n.1, says that these fairs, held four times a year, drew crowds of from 5,000 to 6,000 foreign merchants. The bustle of such a fair is suggested by the print of the much smaller fair at Guibray near Falaise in 1658: Hitzer, *Die Strasse,* pl. 229.

12. Published by the Société de Topographie Historique de Lyon, 1882. [LF]

13. See Ulysse Robert, *Philibert de Chalon, Prince d'Orange, Vice-Roi de Naples* (Paris, 1902). [LF]

14. For details see the useful work of E. Levasseur, *Mémoire sur les monnaies du règne de François I* (Paris, 1902).

[LF] See also Frank C. Spooner, *International Economy and Monetary Movements in France, 1493–1725* (Cambridge, Mass., 1972).

15. *Le Recueil des ordonnances des Pays-Bas,* 2d ser., *1506–1700,* ed. Ch. Laurent and J. La Meere (Brussels, 1898) [LF], II, 103–104.

16. Illustrations of the obviously uneven shape and size of these coins can be found in both Levasseur, *Mémoire,* and Spooner, *International Economy.* Levasseur, p. xxiv, was able to test the weight of gold écus minted in the sixteenth century, when the legal minimum weight for such a coin was 3.398 gm. Forty-two coins obtained from one source weighed an average 3.36 gm. Eighteen coins obtained from another source weighed an average 3.34 gm. The merchants had done their work well.

For the modern American living in a check and charge-card economy, money is an abstraction. In the sixteenth century, it was a given weight of precious metal. Alongside the coins bearing the king's image there were many others in circulation in France, foreign coins and domestic provincial ones. The most important tool of the merchant-banker was his gold-weighing scales.

17. Jean Bodin, *La République,* "Le Moyen d'empescher que les monnoyes soyent altérées de prix ou falsifiées."

18. The Latin Union was a monetary agreement in force from 1865 until World War I between France, Belgium, Italy, and Switzerland, declaring a uniform ratio of the value of silver to gold (1:15.5) in all the member countries of the union.

19. Guillaume Pyet, chancellor of France, responded to a call for all patriotic citizens to donate household silver to be melted into coins with a gift of 302 pounds of silver (the equivalent of about 3,400 modern tablespoons).

20. Adolf Soetbeer, *Edelmetall Produktion und Wertverhältnis zwischen Gold und Silber seit der Entdeckung Amerikas bis zur Gegenwart* (Gotha, 1879), pp. 120–127; for the French ratios see p. 125. Soetbeer notes that in merchants' accounts no distinction is made between precious metals received as coin and in other forms, as dust for example. See also Earl J. Hamilton, *American Treasure and the Price Revolution in Spain* (Cambridge, Mass., 1934), p. 71.

21. France, like other countries, did what it could to attract and keep precious metals within its borders. In the second half of the century a royal ordinance declared that one-third of the precious metal brought into France for the Lyon fairs must remain in the country. Lapeyre, *Une Famille de marchands,* p. 445. Spooner, *International Economy,* p. 117, suggests that by around 1560 the balance in France had shifted, favoring silver over gold. See also Braudel, *The Mediterranean,* I, 472–474.

22. *Réponse de Jean Bodin à Monsieur de Malestroict,* ed. Henri Hauser (Paris, 1932; reprint of 1568 ed.), p. 13.

23. See H. Longchay, "Recherches sur l'origine et la valeur des ducats et des écus espagnols," *Bulletin de l'Académie Royale de Belgique,* classe des lettres, 1906. [LF] The mines of Potosi in "Peru," modern Bolivia, produced prodigious quantities of exceptionally pure silver.

24. Levasseur, *Mémoire,* p. clxxii. Hamilton, *American Treasure,* p. 40, suggests that precious metals arrived in Europe from the New World in the following ratios of gold to silver: 1503—1520, 100 percent to 0 percent; 1521–1530, 97 percent to 3 percent; 1531–1540, 12.5 percent to 87.5 percent; 1541–1560, 15 percent to 85 percent. Although the Potosi mines were discovered in 1545, there is some question today about when coins minted from Potosi silver actually made their appearance in Europe. Braudel, *The Mediterranean,* I, 476, suggests that real quantities of silver did not come from Potosi before the 1570s.

25. Fernand de Mely, "Signatures de Primitifs: Le Banquier et sa femme de Quinten Matsys," *Mélanges offerts à M. Emile Picot* (Paris, 1913), II, 505–514. The painting Febvre describes is reproduced in this article, p. 508. See also Leo van Puyvelde, "Un Portrait de marchand par Quentin Metsys et les percepteurs d'impôts par Marin van Reymervale," *Revue Belge d'archéologie et d'histoire d'art,* 26 (1957), p. 323ff. Jost Aman's engraving is reproduced in part in Coornaert, *Les Français et le commerce international à Anvers,* II, pl, 4, facing p. 136.

26. *Les Compagnies du corail* (Paris, 1908). [LF]

27. The écu d'or soleil, taking its name from a small sun near the edge of the design, was the basic gold coin of the period. About an inch in diameter, it is the coin most often

mentioned when money is being measured in coin rather than money of account. Illustrations in Spooner, *International Economy,* pl. 3, facing p. 152; Levasseur, *Mémoire,* following p. xii.

28. (I cannot find the source of the arithmetical error here.) How reasonable the hypothetical example seems when compared to the Fugger fortune, admittedly exceptional, which produced an average annual profit between 1511 and 1527 of 54.5 percent. Richard Ehrenberg, *Capital and Finance in the Age of the Renaissance,* trans. H. M. Lucas (New York, n.d.), p. 85.

29. On the effects of the Church's stand on usury on those lending money for profit see John T. Noonan, *The Scholastic Analysis of Usury* (Cambridge, Mass., 1957).

30. Martin Wolfe discusses the fiscal concept of and expectations from the king in *The Fiscal System of Renaissance France,* especially chap. 1, "Medieval and Renaissance Fiscal Systems."

31. By his death in 1559 the total debt of Henri II amounted to between 36 and 44 million livres. Lapeyre, *Une Famille,* p. 440. Even more remarkable than the stunning size of the debt is the degree of uncertainty—the whereabouts of some 8 million livres are in question. Under such circumstances it is not surprising that monarchs actually declared bankruptcy—in France, for example, in 1557, in Spain in 1575, and not for the last time.

32. *Revue d'histoire de Lyon,* 9 (1912), pp. 81–102. [LF] The case of Cleberger (or Kleberger, 1486–1546) is an instructive one. He earned the epithet "good German" for his charitable contributions which were made anonymously during his lifetime. He made the first contribution—500 livres, a huge sum—to the fund established in 1531 to provide bread for the poor in times of scarcity. By his death he had contributed nearly 5,000 livres to charitable causes, for which his will provided another 4,000. He earned all this and a good bit more by trade and by lending money at interest. Cleberger was one of those to whom François I turned repeatedly to negotiate loans from the Swiss and German banking community of Lyon, 12,500 écus in 1518, 17,000 in 1522, 13,000 in 1545. These loans were made at 4 percent per fair (that is, 16 percent per annum), the highest rate

permitted foreigners (Frenchmen had lower limits). Cleberger was a native German, but the subjects of the emperor were not always kindly treated in France, a country which was often at war with the emperor. He became a naturalized Frenchman, but, so as not to lose the advantages accorded foreigners doing business at the Lyon fairs, he also became a citizen of Bern.

33. Ehrenberg, *Capital and Finance,* p. 80. Jacob Fugger wrote the emperor: "It is well known your Majesty would not have gained the crown save with mine aid."

34. On all this see Alfred Spont, *Semblançay* (?–1537): La *Bourgeoisie financière au début du seizième siècle* (Paris, 1895), a respectable book if somewhat too thin. [LF] Wolfe, *The Fiscal System,* contains much of this information in "The Semblançay Episode," pp. 67–77.

35. Cardinal Balue rose from humble beginnings to the position intendent des finances under Louis XI. In the course of negotiations between France and Burgundy he was entrusted with a considerable sum of money, much of which went into his own pocket. When this and similar acts came to light he was stripped of all civil duties and placed in one of Louis XI's iron cages at Loches in 1469. Commines, historian and adviser to Louis XI, was disgraced in 1484 when he sided with the wrong faction after the death of the king.

36. Perpignan, capital of Roussillon, was French under Louis XI. French control of the province was challenged by the king of Aragon. He eventually used the province to secure a loan from the French.

37. Charles VIII, as heir to the House of Anjou, had a claim on the old Angevin kingdom which included Naples. The Naples war of 1494–95 resulted in short-lived French control of that province.

38. The *taille* was a general tax on all the property owned by commoners. Noblemen were exempt as were the bourgeois of certain privileged cities. The rate of the *taille* varied from year to year and from province to province, depending on the success of each province in modifying the king's original request. *Aides* were a kind of sales tax. Again the rate varied according to local traditions. The tax, generally levied on meat and drink, was arranged so as to spare the

very poor—transactions of less than a minimum sum were tax-free—and the well-to-do—venison, meat of the nobles, and spices were not taxed. The *gabelle* was a tax on salt, levied when it was transported or sold. Until the end of the century the *gabelle* brought in only between 4 and 10 percent of the total royal revenues; then it rose suddenly bringing in 25 percent. For the way in which it was levied see J. Russell Major, *Representative Institutions in Renaissance France, 1421–1559* (Madison, Wis., 1960). See also Wolfe, *The Fiscal System*, appendix G, "Levying the Tailles," pp. 304–316; appendix H, "Farming the Aides," pp. 317–329; appendix I, "The Salt Taxes," pp. 330–342. For more on the generals of finance see Wolfe, *Fiscal Systems*, pp. 68ff.

39. The official whose duties included running the salt-storage warehouse (the *grenier*) and collecting the *gabelle* was the *grenetier*.

40. We can see this system in action in an entry in a sixteenth-century journal. "The king had promised [Henri d'Estienne] a thousand crowns for his book, *De la précellence du langage François*. The treasurer [from whom he tried to collect] mocked him, and offered him 600. D'Estienne refused and offered him 50 if he would hand over the rest . . . he ran hither and yon trying to collect . . . had finally to return to the same man, to whom he offered 400 if he could take the rest . . . but the other laughed at him and . . . the upshot was that he lost everything." Pierre de l'Estoile, *The Paris of Henry of Navarre*, ed. and trans. Nancy Lyman Roelker (Cambridge, Mass., 1958), p. 112 (July 1585).

Index

155

157

Index

Index